Springtime in Nangaku

Further Adventures with Japanese Chicks

Josh Muggins

Petty Pace Press

ISBN: 978-0-9907464-2-3

Josh Muggins is the author of *How To Pick Up Japanese Chicks And Doom Your Immortal Soul*, *Summer of Marv*, and *Wussie: In Praise of Spineless Men* as well as several magazine features on life in Japan. Throughout the twenty-first century he has ranked among the giants of prose humor in the space between his ears. He can be reached at joshmuggins@hotmail.com, and, for reasons known only to him and his Maker, insists on blogging at joshmuggins.com.

Oh geez, here we go with the disclaimer again

This is a work of fiction, I guess. Oh, I don't know. Reader, if this is your first go-round with me, please understand that I go through this same rigmarole every time. And every time, I say to myself, "By God, Scout (pet name for spleen), I'm going with the nonfiction label on this one!" only to implode at the last second like the Red Viper of Dorne.

To be sure, I have given it the old college try once again re avoiding embellishment, putting recollections onto the page honestly, etc. (Names and descriptive details are altered, as always.) I guess it comes down to how much we can trust memory. Because sometimes we all want to *believe* so strongly that something really happened that we talk ourselves into it. Just open your New Testament, and you're clobbered right off the bat with four starkly differing accounts of, like, the most important things that ever happened. And it turns out there's a slew of *other* gospels out there consigned by the Gatekeepers to self-publishing hell. (Thomas, I feel your pain.)

The point being: you *can't* really trust your memory. Heck, if folks can't keep the contents of the Sermon on the Mount straight—*sainted* folks, at that—how am I supposed to remember the exact flow of conversation that time I had to scold Ruriko and Kimi for erotically yawning in my apartment? That was over two decades ago, for heaven's sake.

I can't document most of the anecdotes that make up this book, and I lack the gene that enables certain bestselling memoirists to market obvious fiction as fact, as well as the other one that provides talent.

So (sigh...) put me down for fiction again.

Crap. Let's just move on.

.

I'M JOSH AND I'LL BE
YOUR AUTHOR THIS EVENING

As we passed on, it seemed as if those scenes of visionary enchantment would never have an end.

– Meriwether Lewis

A few summers back, my wife, who spends most of her time living some six hours distant from me in her native region of rural western Japan (and if you were married to me, you'd most likely want six hours of distance between us, too), came to see me in Yokohama, where—through no fault of my own, I assure you—I hold the position of associate professor of English at a private university.

The purpose of her visit was dental, not conjugal. After nearly three decades of marriage, we're beyond that sort of nonsense, at least with regard to each other. There is a noted specialist here in town whom she needed to consult.

The subway trip to the clinic took us through a stretch of the city that I had not traversed in several years, and involved a transfer

1

at the very station near which stands fabled N. University—the school that employed me through all of the Nineties and most of the Aughts.

A pretty young woman also boarded at this station and sat opposite us. She was fashionable in an understated way and careful of her appearance, and she radiated a cool, confident intelligence. I whispered to Mrs. Muggins, "I'll bet she's a Nangaku girl!"—Nangaku being a sort of abbreviation for NU, except that it's not because I am changing all names here including my own.

Mrs. Muggins knew where I was heading and said, in the tone of a mother explaining to an obese seven-year-old why we would not be stopping for ice cream, "But she wouldn't know who you are."

She was right, of course. Even if I had worked up the nerve to introduce myself and confirm that our fellow passenger was indeed a denizen of that fabled institution, my name would hold no meaning. To her, I would register as nothing more than an addled, cleavage-dazed coot who avoided being considered a threat only by virtue of age and the presence of a female Japanese caretaker. And she, too, would be right.

It was a crushing revelation. For I, like fellow American depressive Meriwether Lewis, had once been allowed, through the grace of God, to view ongoing scenes of visionary enchantment, albeit it of a very different sort, and I, too, deluded myself into believing, for a time, that they would never have an end, and yet have an end they did, and, as I'm sure Meriwether would tell you if he could, boy, does it suck ass when you wake up one day and find that you're shit out of visionary enchantment.

September 2015

The Greatest Generation

Beauty and folly are old companions.

– Benjamin Franklin

Notwithstanding the potentially devastating breakdown of my air conditioner, the party I was hosting for my new college friends was going smashingly well. I might even have been able to relax but for the voluptuous blonde eighteen-year-old trying to pull my pants off.

Kiko and I were among the twelve participants sitting in a circle on the tatami floor of my sweltering bedroom, sipping beer and cocktails as we waited for the latecomers. She had insisted that I sit by her, and in retrospect, the white shorts with the elastic waistband were a tragic fashion choice. Every time I stood up, Kiko grabbed for the cuff of one or both legs and yanked, exposing my purple briefs (another regrettable choice) with varying degrees of success. And if she ever did get the shorts all the way down, I harbored no delusions that she would stop there.

Good lord, it's only five-thirty on a school night, I marveled. *How did we get to this point so soon?*

—◻—

I had skipped my classes at NU that day just to be home to let the air-con repairman in. The thing had died on me two days earlier, rendering the atmosphere of the rooms downright Venusian—an environment uncomfortable even for a chap living alone, and certainly not one into which you would want to inject a couple dozen excitable Japanese freshmen.

But the repair dude, still there as the first wave of guests arrived, muttered something about ordering a part and coming back on Thursday. I consulted with the lovely, saucer-eyed Nanako as to what we should do—perhaps move the event to a bar?—but she insisted that everyone would gladly tough it out.

My journal informs me that...

I immediately fled to the store to buy sushi and ice cream (at Nanako's request) and an electric fan (mainly for my own survival, but let them think it was for them).

The fan was greeted with great joy. In the meantime, more had arrived, including Kiko Kogawa. She proved herself ideal wife material. In my absence, she had cleaned up my filthy refrigerator. She immediately set about assembling the fan. She fixed me overly strong gin-and-tonic cocktails. She prepared a seat for me next to her in front of the sushi. Later on, upon hearing about my famously dirty microwave, she even took a semi-successful stab at cleaning it. And all this she did while continuously displaying spectacular cleavage from numerous original angles. She was great.

July 2002

Re-reading this many years on, I wonder what those "original angles" were. I had known Kiko only three months by this time but liked to think myself the world's foremost scholar of her cleavage. I could easily have cranked out a ten-page paper on the subject and a couple of haikus on the side. Perhaps she was offering side-boob on this occasion. That would have been new.

My recollection of her cocktails is more vivid. I was well into my second one when I realized that Kiko interpreted "gin-and-tonic" as literally equal parts gin and tonic.

—◻—

The apartment was immense for one person by Japanese standards: something on the order of 330 square feet divided into three main rooms. The traditional sliding *shoji* that separated the carpeted living room and the tatami bedroom had been removed prior to the arrival of guests, mainly to create a larger space but also to avoid the scenario in which a liquored-up freshman boy might plow through one of those antique paper doors, leaving a Wile E. Coyote-falling-through-clouds outline. I knew my people well.

I resided on the upper floor of a two-story wooden building, meaning that a party of this sort was certain to bedevil the downstairs neighbors no end. But whatever concern I felt for my neighbors was back-burnered while I fended off my own personal bedeviler, Kiko. By no means was I philosophically opposed to having my pants pulled down by perhaps the most beguiling freshman girl in the entire International Relations Department; it was just that I would have preferred not having it done in front of a live and increasingly rowdy audience.

It occurred to me to take Kiko aside for a private showing. There was a risk of scandal associated with this notion—with just making the offer—but that risk was minimized by the probability that I would be leaving NU at the end of the academic year anyway. And it would make for a great story. I allowed my mind to play out the scenario while the others prattled away, oblivious to my presence, just like in class.

The laundry/bath area would have been the proper venue, as it could be curtained off. Kiko would not say no, but would likely insist on bringing a friend. That honor would probably fall on Nanako, which was fine with me. I'd developed a profound affection for Nanako—not one that had heretofore manifested itself in a desire to expose myself to her, but I found myself warming to the idea after a couple of Kiko's customized cocktails.

—◻—

In case I've failed to make it clear, I was the English teacher of these freshmen. From the outset of the Japanese academic year in April 2002 I had been meeting them ninety minutes per day, four mornings per week to teach them reading, writing, speaking, and listening.

Now, it's not entirely out of the question for a forty-six-year-old man to be attractive to college women. My age peers Bruce Willis (just a few years removed from *The Sixth Sense* at this time) and Kevin Costner (a few years removed from nothing he wants cited) come to mind. But me? I was clearly not the product of a Hollywood personal trainer.

Oh, I worked out when I had the chance and kept my weight around one-forty and took a few borderline-metrosexual grooming measures to appear younger than my true age, notably shaving my face, head, and torso to eliminate telltale gray hair. But I had no chest at all, and my white, spindly legs were a source of much merrymaking at this party. Physically, the only feature I took pride in was the one I'd just chosen not to put on display.

Surely, then, you say, I must have been a *wealthy* forty-six-year-old. Not so. I had limited personal savings, I rented my apartment, I had no car. I could be generous with groups of students, such as by footing the bill for most of the non-liquid party refreshments, but I never lavished gifts on any individual.

So, power was my aphrodisiac? *Hoh, hoh,* if only. I was then on a limited contract at NU. It afforded me a private office and semiannual bonuses, but no chance of tenure and no seat at any faculty meetings. I had the power to give my students failing grades, of course, which could somewhat inconvenience them. But the semester was winding down in July 2002, and everyone at this party had already been informed that they had passed.

What's more, the regular faculty in my department made much of student feedback when deciding on contract renewals for my ilk, so in terms of power, the proverbial shoe was on the other foot here.

Oh, and there's this, too: I was (and still am, at this writing) married, though living apart from my wife. Like a great many married men in Japan, I wear no ring, but neither do I keep my status a secret.

So just what was it that made gorgeous young women feel perfectly at ease waltzing into my home and trying to pull my pants off? Don't you wish you knew?

I don't. I used to. Oh, my, yes, I used to sit up late formulating theories ("It's one of those *Truman Show* conspiracies!"), but ultimately decided that it was like decoding why certain jokes are funny and thereby stripping them of funniness. Best to leave some things alone and just accept them. Beautiful Japanese teens pulling down your pants? I chose to embrace the mystery.

Meanwhile, back at that party...

—▢—

Aika Matsuo arrived late, which was no surprise, with her usually prompt friend Kazumi. They declared my shirtless body not adequate for their minimal standards. I immediately challenged them to a Scott Helvenston Navy Seals workout. They barely made it through the pushup section (but so did I), and crapped out during the abdominals. I can't believe I led five people in simultaneous jumping jacks. I want to set myself on fire in front of the neighbors...

July 2002

My journal is mum on the question of how I ended up shirtless. A benighted attempt to negotiate a treaty of reciprocity with Kiko, perhaps. One detail that I do recall, though, was a demonstration of my abdominal strength that involved having Kazumi stand on my naked stomach.

Perhaps five-four and about a hundred ten pounds, Kazumi planted one foot and then the other on my abdomen. Two classmates who had seized her arms gradually relaxed their grip, transferring her entire weight onto me, which I bore coolly for all of seven seconds before tromboning a B-flat-to-F-glissando fart.

My topless ab-flaunting ploy took place on the living room floor, with me on essentially the same spot where I had awakened precisely two years earlier from a failed suicide attempt brought on by a relationship gone sour with an International Relations major. But that is a whole 'nother story.*

It seemed they would stay, but while I showered, they decided to leave. I missed them, but slept soundly despite the heat. In the morning, I found somebody's pants. I still have no idea whose.

July 2002

I propose this as a cultural universal: It's always a sign of a successful party when there are Mystery Pants.

—◻—

What could be more delightful for an untalented forty-six-year-old white man than to have such a charming and exciting coterie of friends? I mean, it sure beats fending off irrelevancy by starring in *The Postman* and *Waterworld*. But the one thing that could be better, I suppose, is having *two* such charming and exciting coteries of friends, as I did.

The *other* freshman group, whom I also taught four mornings a week, held their semester-end party a few nights later. They took the more traditional route of reserving a private tatami-matted room in one of the local bars that cater to students below the legal drinking age.

I kissed Kan Sezaki on the lips—my second boy in a little over a week. The big-titted and sexy Yayoi wanted me to take her to Hawaii... She seemed

---

* One available on Amazon, I hasten to add.

9

to want to come home with me right then and there, too, although the fact that she dragged Tsuneo Moriyama along with her to my bus stop indicates that she didn't have anything too sinister in mind. Anyway, I said no. It was too soon after the wild goings-on with the other freshman group. I apologized to the landlady about that one.

There was the usual inane chugging and mindless yelling. I was in my element. I tastefully consoled Izumi Hatayama about her dead boyfriend between shots of chilled saké. I declared my love (again) for Etsuko Furukawa who, a few days earlier, had arrived at school at 6:30 a.m. to stand first in line [to sign up] *for my September TOEFL class. But it turns out that Etsuko is hooked up with a fortune teller who is (gasp!) ten years her senior.*

July 2002

One month earlier, Near Earth Asteroid 2002 MN had missed our planet by 75,000 miles, a mere one-third the distance to the moon. I, for one, was glad. I wouldn't have missed those parties for the world.

The Faithful Correspondent

It is one of the blessings of old friends that you can afford to be stupid with them.

—Ralph Waldo Emerson

Someone live with his/her husband/wife, on the other hand, others don't. I talked about many kinds of married with a 25 years old Assie guy whom i meet often these days. He doesn't like being all the time with wife or gf. I agree.

I think it is natural that i shouldn't tell Misako that you sleep with imagining her naked, so i don't and I won't. I don't wanna break you and her strong friendship(?). So i won't. But i can listen what you imagine! Don't hegitate----!

One question: Is it strange to have sex friends? and Do I look easy????Actually these days I'm sooo famous.i mean I am asked to have sex by some guys. (included Japanese guys and Assie guy,too.) so I'm wondering if i look "easy". I don't say i hate sex, but if i am regarded as a "easy woman", i don't do that anymore.

By the way, actually I'm supposed to meet that Aussie guy at nite in the car at the restaurant today. I don't know whether we have a sexual relation.(but he is soooo player, i guess and he said he had 5 Japanese gfs before. How do you feel??

Oh I've got to go now!

12

Bye bye.
your sweet Kotoko

In the summer vacation months following those freshman parties, I taught two six-day intensive courses for the purpose of preparing NU students for the TOEFL, the standardized English test used by many Western universities to screen foreign applicants. In one of these, I encountered for the first time this Kotoko, a brilliant International Relations junior who had somehow eluded detection for the first two and a half years of her NU career.

After the course, she started trawling for advice about her application to the exchange program, occasionally via office visits but more often by email. Things started off prudently enough, as things are wont to do, but soon the center could not hold.

Every time i buy Cosmo,i hasitate to bring it to the cach corner coz I'm afraid of being considered I'm horny.haha!... Contents of Cosmo are about how to attract guys and how to make love nicely(?)..And about fashion a little and it has a lot of advertisements.

mmm,how about writing email to you almost everyday?? (actually,I'm enjoying writing you a e-mail everyday about study abroad and other things...hehe)

P.s Is anyone who calls you Joshua?I really like your name.

—◻—

We got her settled on Victoria in New Zealand as her first choice and she passed the selection process the following spring. In the meantime, she wrote…

Do you like talking about love?! I love to!

…and soon thereafter:

First, i didn't stay at his house last nite! But i ended up........(guess)
I knew you are NOT *jealous* AT ALL *and don't regard me as a*
woman, so...... '(I don't know what do i wanna talk about....above my head.)

I'm confident in the safty during sex since i have sexed for the first
time.I'm into safe sex. No glove,no love. This is my belief. Pregnancy is too
risky for me and scary. If I was pregnant now,my dream of studying abroad
would go away and the chance would never come.

I don't get angry at your email at all except the description about my
breasts. According to Japanese guys, they seem to big, BUT BUT *for*
foreigners, they seem to a kinda small but well-shaped. I don't like to be said
they are big, i don't know why i feel that way, but this is strange fact. Maybe i
don't wanna be the subject to be seen as a woman and to be used as a tool of
enjying for guys unknowingly.

It was untrue that I did not "regard her as a woman." This was,
I suppose, her way of registering faux disappointment at my failure
to be aroused by her. It wasn't for lack of trying on my part…

Yes, i love you too! Do you know how much your coments written on the
answer sheet of the last TOEFL *class's whole test, encouraged me!*
Besides,these days, by telling what happend to me and what i think to you,i feel
really relaxed and relieved. You are my speacial.

…and yet, the sparks never really flew. Not the sparks of lust,
anyway. I myself found my lack of lechery curious, and certainly it
had nothing to do with her appearance, which was striking. Her
piercingly intelligent, dark almond eyes were what leapt out at me,
though aficionados of lush and wavy jet-black hair or flawless
cheekbones or translucent skin could cite these marvels as well. She
cut a fine figure, too, with breasts that were, as advertised, pert and
well-shaped. And yet… And yet…

I would look at her during those visits to my office and think, *It's the darnedest thing! Objectively, this is someone that I should be masturbating to on a regular basis.* And yet, I could never manage to work her into the rotation.* She was like reverse kryptonite to me, the only naturally occurring female substance on the campus that *didn't* leave me weak-kneed and vulnerable.

Evidently, she felt it, too:

> *Since we began to email so often, strangely,when i meet you in campus,i feel something embarrecing. Do you understand what I'm trying to convey?? Thanks to email,i can say everything i wanna tell you without shyness. ;)*
>
> *See ya !*

Your cutie,
Kotoko

I did understand. It was damned awkward running into her at, say, the campus ATM the morning after a steamy exchange. And so, by mutual tacit consent, ours became purely an email relationship. I satisfied her need for unvarnished insights into the male psyche while she slaked my need to talk dirty to a pretty NU girl. And so a cybernetic friendship bloomed.

> *One question to you: why many foreigners like Japanese girls and why do that like Japanese girls' looking? I am said "you are really beautiful" by foreign guys in the chat on the web or in person. Are they just compliments?*
>
> *I love watching "Ally Mcbeal" (American TV drama, you must know it) and of course i watch that every Sunday. In addition,i rent some videos of Ally*

---

* The backlog of girls who deserved to be masturbated to at NU was a constant source of pressure in those years. "Oh, I've never given Aya the solo scene she deserves!" etc. Little did I realize that there would be loads of time to catch up once I went into exile. Thank God I kept all the pictures.

from time to time. I can study many things about love!!!I like it.

Ally said,it's too eary to make love on the first date. I agree.Do you think so??? But i guess, men don't think so. My ex-Ausiie bf tried to sex with me on the first date at his apartment.(but we didn't cause i thought it's too eary then).Also,Ally's bf tried to do that on the first day of dating. mmmmmmmmmmm..........of course it's not like i hate sex,but perhaps,I'm afraid of being treated lightly.I wanna be cherished and treated as an important person.That's all...

—◻—

HI Joshua,

Why did you title "Evil thoughts" in your last email???
Masturbating...???? I heard from Greg that every man needs to masturbate. But i can't imagine every man around me does that...

And,antually i met a guy last night after the concert. I met him on the web and he said to me hi first in the chat. He is Japanese-Spanish and from Uruguay. He really likes me and i also thought he is nice while we were talking on the phone. He looks like Japanese, but he can't speak Japanese. He can speak English and Spanish. (Spanish is main language for him. I can speak Spanish a little bit because i had been studying it for 1 year in my high school.

I could learn many many important things [in high school] as a woman and a person.We didn't learn about men, though. We were taught that we have to pay attention when we choose man and go out with men.

—◻—

All too soon came her departure for New Zealand. There ensued one of those alarming Apollo 13-like radio silences, but she resumed our correspondence once she had settled in. By this time, like many an NU girl before her who had found herself in a multiethnic environment, she was learning to cope with a sudden surge in popularity.

Another HOng Kong guy told me he likes me a bit the other day...and i think he has nice personality and he is kind person not like previous Hong Kong guy,so these days we were really close and had "a" relationship. I tried to love him,but "something is different". He is not so handsome,but not agly. He is pretty tall and intelligent.But somehow.....probably i couldn't enjoy sex with him (his size is too big for me. ..it was really painful. I haven't felt "painful" during sex,but it was. I think physical relation is verry important for lasting relationship,so i think I should leave him before he begins love me so much (he likes me,but he doesn't love me yet.).......and ....Now i wanna be by myself and don't wanna think about guys ...i'm rally busy with assignment and thinking about my future.... I really wanna stay here and live here in the fuutre.I wish i could get job here...i knew it's really difficult though...

That's it. By the way i got A in history paper the other day! Studying here is so far so good. Teachers are really ambitious and nice to me :)Friends are nice to me as well.

How is your life going?

My own lack of attraction for her, I came to understand, was simply a function of awe. Not only had she blithely accumulated vastly more sexual experience in half my years, but she was padding her lead on a weekly basis. Though she wasn't deliberately showboating, she was gradually making me feel like the Washington Generals of sex.

Whereas other NU fantasy objects perhaps could have compared my hypothetical sex-having prowess to one or two predecessors, Kotoko was capable of grading me on a hundred-point scale—maybe even with a decimal point. It was the idea of that decimal point above all other things that made me shudder. I kept writing back, though.

Ok ok,Actully i had a physical relationship the other day(3days ago..)But!!!I'm worried again.This time not about length, but "time"..

He finished very fast.Around....2 minutes..?I was surprised and a little bit shocked because i couldn't enjoy it at all...It was like "Oh? Already?" BUt i know girls aren't supposed to say "You come so fast(or already?)"and "what are you thinking about now?"so,i didn't say anything.....

Some ideas came up with me....the reasons are must be....

1.He hadn't masturbated for a long time or hadn't had sex in ages
2.He turned on too much because i was too sexy
3.Physically he is easy to come

If it's 3, that's a bit problem...Some friends had told me guys can overcome by training not to come fast.But we have only 4months left, so i wanna enjoy with him as soon as possible.

Well, anyway, I'll wait and see the next time..If the same thing will happen,I'll worried again..What do you think???I'm serious.

The first draft of my response began, "Well, what do you want *me* to do about it?" I supposed I could fly down there and sit in the room and stare during the whole proceeding. The unexplained presence of a silent, older, bald gentleman in the corner might provide about the right degree of buzzkill; I knew it would have worked for me.

Instead, I just got to waxing nostalgic about my own experience with premature ejaculation, and had ejaculated nearly two thousand words on the topic before I knew what was what.

But do you see? Do you see what she did there? Do you see how this sort of email made actual sexual contact between her and me unthinkable?

Because, might she not share her disappointing experience vis-à-vis me with some other correspondent? And me, never the wiser? Don't you just hate people who take it upon themselves to bare all their sexual liaisons to all and sundry without getting their partners' permission? Is there any lower form of life slithering on the earth? But I digress.

— ☐ —

Thanks for your a heap of advice!And actually.....you know what?We tried it again and it was ok yesterday morning!(Actually we tried 2 days ago at night but he wanted to come fast again,so i let him come.And we decied to do that the next morning again.)

The second time, there was no problem :) It was before I read your last email,but your advice will be our help.(I won't tell him anything, though)He looked satisfied after our second try. We thanked to each other :P

It occurs to me that I could just cobble together one of those "Shit My So-and-so Says" books from my over 100,000-word correspondence with Kotoko, finish before lunch, and have a far more marketable product than the one I'm slaving over now. But as Richard Nixon was fond of saying, "It would be wrong."[*]

So let us leave Kotoko and her cheerful, oblivious, prolifically ejaculating paramour-du-jour for the time being, secure in the knowledge that I can always chuck in some more excerpts whenever things bog down.

---

[*] According to a team of ethicists laboring deep inside my butt, it is perfectly okay to publish without permission a *fraction* of one's ancient email history with another individual (assuming ample identity cloaking, sufficient passage of time, etc.), but way out of bounds to quote *most* of any particular history.

Other People's Daughters

There are several good protections against temptation, but the surest is cowardice.

—Mark Twain

I don't want to screw up these freshmen classes... Life couldn't possibly be better than it has been of late inside an NU classroom with the doors closed. If only I could just go to a class on a nice Thursday morning and stay in there forever...

But I have to come out and face harsh realities, like the need for outside work, the inevitability of the end of the road coming at NU, and so on.

May 2002

I had known that a beady-eyed junior boy, Yasushi, was fond of me ever since his attempt to slide his tongue down my throat during my birthday party the previous year. Now he was putting together an all-male team for an intramural volleyball tournament and begging me to join it. I agreed on condition that we call the team the Fighting Bedwetters, but caved and joined anyway when he pocket-vetoed my proposal.

Then on Wednesday, I was roped into the volleyball tournament at the gym by old kissing buddy Yasushi Senda. We (the "Psycho Drivers," as Yasushi insisted on naming us) were 4-2 overall, including a first-round forfeit by the

"Lovely Girls." Two of our other victories came over groups consisting mainly of freshman girls, who refused to engage in the traditional World Cup shirt exchange with me after the matches. There were moments of utter humiliation, and even more moments of pain, as I badly twisted my ankle in practice before we got our first shot off. But it was worth it. I had fun.

June 2002

—☐—

To walk into an NU classroom full of International Relations freshmen circa 2002 was to wade into a tsunami of catastrophic cuteness. That is the first thing you would notice. The wallop of that concentrated cuteness uppercuts a middle-aged white man right in the middle-aged white nuts.

Spend a semester with those freshmen—six hours a week in class, plus uncounted hours poring over their homework, plus mandatory "friendly" exchanges of English email, plus the occasional marathon party that may very well result in persons partially or totally losing their pants—and you obtain something of a broader perspective.

Take Rikako over there, the hollow-cheeked, large-eyed waif giving off a sexually mature Wednesday Addams vibe. Turns out she opted to major in International Relations in order to research the problems of homelessness and child labor in the Philippines, and made not one but two trips there to assess the situation on the ground while still in high school.

Or Nanako, that tanned, bubbly little genius in the front row. As student council president in her junior high school—*junior* high school!—she proposed and rammed through a policy…well, she can speak for herself:

Foster Program is to be the foster Parents for hunger Child and to go to school. That plan was passed by universal request.

And Nanako was still in office when the first beneficiary, a girl

22

from Cambodia, arrived at her school.

Yasuko, she of the almond-shaped head and parabolic eyebrows, devoted the spring vacation before her first semester to playing with poor children in Nepal, then spent part of the summer touring Mongolia. Prior to the start of her second year, she would co-found a world-hunger-fighting club with the equally adorable Yayoi and a male classmate. She also found time to go to the Britney Spears arena concert at Tokyo Dome that year.

The statuesque Mika spent the Saturday nights of her freshman year volunteering to teach Japanese to children of underprivileged immigrants; and you know, I could go on and on and on with these examples, which represent but a fraction of one International Relations cohort that was by no means atypical...

I don't know about you, but I spindle my brain trying to dredge up a single instance of a time during my teen years when I gave even a moment's thought to the poors of foreign lands, as seemed to come so naturally to Nangaku freshman girls. On top of that, most of them lived apart from their families at age eighteen in studio apartments (there being no dorms), worked long hours to save money for further trips to impoverished lands during school vacations, and took turns protecting each other when one of their number drank too heavily.

Thus, the idea of a "maturity gap"—that "Oh, they're just kids, for God's sake! Other people's daughters!"—never really impeded my self-gratification endeavors.

—◻—

This is not to say that every NU girl was a selfless angel sent to shame my ilk. Kiko, the voluptuous pants-grabber and lethal cocktail-mixer, spent every minute of class chattering with her friends and every extracurricular moment polishing hiphop dance moves with her crew right smack in front of the entrance to the International Relations building.

When, with a few weeks to go in the semester, I dusted off my semiannual more-in-sadness-than-in-anger speech declaring that "some in this room" were not going to pull out a passing grade as things stand now, everyone present knew that it was primarily directed at Kiko. "I'm not going to name names," I nobly intoned, only to be cut off by Kiko's boosterish sidekick, Ryoko: "Muggins! Muggins! Look! Look!" she burbled, frantically pointing to Kiko, who, having bundled her bosoms in her arms, was now leaning forward to attain maximum cleavage.

"Very nice, Kiko," I muttered, in what I hoped seemed a composed manner, "but I've seen those things a thousand times, and so has every other man on this campus."

—□—

Today, Ai and Yu came by my office at lunch to hang out, shoot some baskets, invite me to go paragliding, and just fart around. That won't happen at AU. Tonight, I went along with Kayo, Yu, Kazumi, Junichi and Tokiko for okonomiya, and let myself get tricked into paying the whole bill. "It comes to 8000 yen each," they told me. Nope, that won't happen at AU, either.

October 2002

By this point in my career, I thought little of forking over large sums of money to pay a disproportionate share of the bill for a night out—or all of the bill, as in this case. I had come to think of it as hush money. Any visit to a restaurant or bar with female IR majors would inevitably result in at least a half-dozen inappropriate utterances on my part, but I knew they wouldn't have the heart to rat me out if I was treating.

I had recently compiled the "Top Ten International Relations Freshmen That I Want to See Naked" ranking. The document was shrouded in secrecy, at least when I was sober, but I freely gave away tidbits whenever Demon Rum loosened my tongue. Ai (#9) and Yu (#3), the wonderful Pronoun Sisters, both made the cut.

"AU" was a university in western Tokyo Prefecture, to which I believed I would be moving at the end of that academic year. I was in the middle of a six-year contract term with International Relations at NU but, owing to political strife with some of the tenured faculty, had determined that I could bear to stay no longer.*

I was in a tight spot job-search-wise, as most universities refused to consider applicants over forty for full-time positions. And then one day I found in my mailbox, amid rejection letters, a flier from a dubious organization seeking to recruit men aged eighteen to forty-eight to be "shutcho hosts."

Half gigolo and half Batman, a shutcho host pilots a hot car to places where neglected housewives wait to pay him for various ministrations. At least one of my male students was so employed.

To summarize, then, I was too old at the time to become a professor, but still just young enough to be a vigilante boy-toy. The old query bears repeating: "Japan: great country, or what?"

I did not pursue the shutcho host option. I suspected they were after men who were less bald, less furry, and less foreign; besides which, the hot car provided would almost certainly be a manual, which is a deal-breaker for me.

—□—

AU didn't care that I was bald and furry and feared the stick-shift, and they loved the fact that I was foreign—and better still, a native English speaker with university teaching experience in Japan. They seldom got applicants like me for the very good reason that their salary was a fraction of what I got at NU. They did offer a free apartment, but with half the floor space of a Depression-era hobo's boxcar. Scarcely enough room, in other words, to pull one's own pants down, let alone bring in a vivacious freshman girl to do it.

---

* In fact, my seventeen-year NU career was only about seventy percent done at the time. "Live every day as if it were your last" was a common Internet bromide then (as now). That philosophy struck me as endlessly tiring, but it was the easiest thing in the world to recklessly live every NU year as if it were the last, since my superiors were thoughtful enough to ensure that I constantly felt that way.

Far more critical than such trivia as salary and shelter, the prospects of meeting vivacious freshman girls of the quality to which I had grown accustomed were dim. I would have economics majors and the like, sluggish, mackerel-brained creatures who waft through the aquarium of academic life rarely responding to external stimuli.

All this I knew, and yet I went forward with the AU interview that fall and was offered a position. With nothing left to lose at NU, I felt free to start rumors about my departure (by showing the shutcho host ad to students and announcing "Tell your moms!"), and free to draw up lists of freshmen girls that I most wanted to see naked, too.

Which were great releases from stress. Still, nary a day went by that I did not note, with head-shaking melancholy, "This shit isn't gonna happen at AU."

—◻—

I'm so-so-so-so-so-shocked at your news that you will not be my home-room teacher next year. We absolutely need you though, why you have to leave from us? Is it impossible to change your decision? I may be take your TOEFL course if I could, it could be a last time to see you?

Mamiko, aka #5

we can learn English pleasantly and develop our own English ability effectively through the grace of the funny and kind character of the teacher. We love our teacher from the bottom of our hearts!! We want to go on being his students forever. We have to stop him from going to be Shutcho host!!

Yasuko, aka #10

Well, they certainly sound sincere in their emails, but I never believed these quick-witted girls were swallowing the shutcho host business. As always in these relationships, you never quite know who is yanking whose chain.

Toward the end of the year, some NU bigwigs got together in a room—to what degree smoke-filled I cannot say—and determined that I be transferred to a newly formed department where I could live out the years of my contract within the university, but at a safe distance from my IR faculty tormentors. I leapt at the offer and broke the hearts of my would-be AU overlords.

—◻—

I had about 18 people here at one time on Monday, including a couple that I didn't even know. Kazumi Ando rummaged through my videos, trying to find the dirty ones, but I had outfoxed her by re-labeling them. Instead she found "My Neighbor Totoro" and insisted on playing it. There was a moment of trepidation during which I wondered if it was, in fact, "Totoro," or had been re-labeled, but to my relief it was indeed "Totoro."

I flirted with the flinty Cow-Island Girl* and told Ai Enoki that I want to see her naked. Toru came, which meant we had no trouble at all consuming seven pizzas, not to mention all other food-stuffs in the house and everything that I had to drink.

After the girls went home, the boys asked me for advice on picking up chicks. They honestly seemed to believe that I could have any of the girls I wanted. They were ashamed, they said, of their tiny penises. I wanted to point out that I also can't succeed in spite of having an enormous penis, but I didn't think it would make them feel better.

I didn't know what else to tell them, so I waxed poetic about the virtues of simply holding a woman, of having a gentle touch. I even taught them the vaginal insertion "telephone dialing" technique...

January 2003

There was always a let-down after these house parties ended when I found myself cleaning up the debris from the table and floor.[†] But in the midst of chucking paper plates and chunks of

---

* A play on the meaning of the Chinese characters that composed her name.

pizza crust and sundry other detritus into a forty-five-liter semi-transparent garbage bag, there was always that chilling moment when a voice inside would say:

This is the future, you know.

And I would say: "You talking to me?"

And the voice would say: *You know I am.*

And I would say: "*What* is the future? *Whose* future?"

Your future, came the answer. *One of these days, you'll be looking at an apartment completely devoid of NU chicks.*

"Hey, that's most days already."

Yes, but most days will soon enough become all *days. And you will have no prospects ever to have any NU chicks in your home. Ever. Again.*

"That's spooky."

Yeah. Like the twin girls in The Shining, *but just the opposite: "We won't come and play with you, Danny. For ever…"*

"'And ever…'"

"And ever." Right.

---

† And winning the right to do that cleaning up was no easy feat. Centuries of breeding conspired to make Japanese girls compulsive cleaner-uppers after parties, no matter how wobbly they may have been themselves. But I would shoo them away, always in the hope that they would think, "What a wonderful husband Muggins would make!" "Yes! Let's fellate him ruthlessly until he weeps blood and cries out for porridge!" But to no avail.

"What a Gloomy Gus you are!"

But I knew he was right. New contract or no, sooner or later, this party would come to an end.

—¤—

The Tuesday night event featured the firing of "crackers" in spite of the fact that we were having nabe *dishes over open flames.* Kan Sezaki was fire-safety-conscious, choosing to shoot three crackers directly into his mouth. No wonder these guys never get laid.†*

I was in fine humorous form, and at one point actually caused the usually ladylike Ayako to spit huge chunks of half-chewed food out of her mouth with laughter. I was proud of that.

Yasuko Hirata, once liquored up, signaled that she was in fact really available for anything I might have in mind, and she is, after all, on the "list" at number ten. I think she has a quasi-boyfriend who is mentally ill, who would suffer mightily if I took away his only decent chance at getting laid, and who lives less than a minute from my house.

January 2003

—¤—

---

* Cracker: a two-inch cardboard cone stuffed full of colorful (and flammable) paper streamers that are spewed into the air upon pulling a string. The party in question took place in a bar, where we ate from traditional communal stew pots (*nabe*) set atop gas burners placed at intervals atop a long table. Thus, it was the office of a responsible adult to stop these rambunctious youngsters from firing flammable paper streamers into the air there, and a shame that we didn't have one.

† And if you scoffed at my cleaning-my-own-house gambit for awakening freshman girls' libidos, imagine the flights of fancy spiraling through Kan's cortex that night.

By the end of the calendar year, my endocrine system had settled on Yayoi, co-founder of the world hunger fighting club. I found her naively noble, engagingly combative, and chestily gifted.

From the very first day of class, a chilly April morning, she had been showing me the goods from a front-row center seat, her alabaster bosoms lolling on her desk like two baby white seals sunning on an ice floe. When I first composed The List, she was #2, and would claim the top spot on my birthday in October.*

Did you surprise yesterday?
I was happy to give the best presents.
May you enjoy this age!

-- *Yayoi*

Dear Yayoi,

Yes, I was surprised and delighted to get your kiss on my birthday! I can't wait to develop the picture. Maybe I will put it on the internet so that millions of Muggins fans can enjoy the scene.

—◻—

I called her on December 24, aka Sex-mas, the holiday on which all boyfriends must take their girls out to a nice dinner as a prelude to a perfunctory trip to a love hotel. The purpose of my call was not to ask her out on such a date but simply to make sure that she wasn't on one.

I also took the opportunity to mention that I was married, just to get that out there, and she already knew. As there had been much banter about movies in our teacher-student email exchanges, I tried to nudge her toward suggesting a date, since I was

---

* The List, it should be noted, was a living document patterned after the U.S. Constitution, forever subject to amendment.

prohibited from making that move by both my status and prodigious wussitude.

The "date" finally materialized in late January, after I had filed grades, making her officially no longer my student, at least in my mind, which was the only place that mattered. She invited her friend Hitoko along and was grumpy and cold throughout, as if I were holding her hostage. I mentally demoted her clear off the list. At least *Gangs of New York* was good.

Two months later, on the eve of a new academic year, there was this:

Yayoi Shimamura suddenly appears to be in heat. After a long cool spell following our crappy date, she's now messaging me right and left (in Japanese). I must strike while the iron is hot.

March 2003

The Iron Cools

Ten years earlier, after a seven-year stab at conventional marital cohabitation, Mrs. Muggins and I realized that we were not that type of human. She opted to return to her hometown in rural western Japan to pursue her creative and entrepreneurial goals while I would remain in the megalopolis and provide financial support through my teaching career.

Before the decision was finalized, there had been this conversation:

Mrs. Muggins: You're going to be okay living alone? I mean, with all those cute NU girls running around?

Me: I swear that I'll never prey upon any of those girls. But, I have to tell you this, in all honesty: If any of *them* should ever decide to prey upon *me*, I would—

Mrs. Muggins: HA-HA-HA-HA-HA-HA-HA-HA-HA!!!!

For the record, I intended to conclude my remarks with "be helpless to resist," but I'm confident that Mrs. Muggins got that, and really did appreciate the futility of my resisting any hypothetical predation at the talons of an NU girl.

And for the record, I held to my vow throughout my NU career. My lone affair with an NU student had not initially been my idea, although I made it clear that I was open to suggestions. If the long, gummy genesis of that doomed relationship could be boiled down to two lines of dialogue, I suppose it would read like this:

Princess Michiko: I say. I wonder if you and I might… I mean, would you by any chance be willing to consider—

Me: Yes! *Yessss!* Ohhhhh, sweet swaying nutsack of Yoda, *yessss!!!*

Okay, so I wasn't exactly "preyed upon." Not technically, I suppose.

Once the trauma of the inevitable breakup with Michiko had worn off, I was back on the sidelines, waving my arms like the scrawniest, runtiest kid trying to get noticed by the captains choosing sides for a pickup basketball game. *Prey upon me! Oh, won't someone please prey upon me? I'll do my best to give satisfaction and shan't be any bother, I swear!*

And finally, one of those captains, this Yayoi, seemed to take pity on me.

She was short and wore her sometimes magenta hair in a style that, perhaps unknown to Yayoi, was then celebrated in the Great Satan as "the Rachel," and her milky-skinned China-doll veneer concealed a mercurial attitude. She seemed to regard our slow, mutual slide toward sin the way she would a persistent cloud of gnats, as something to be tolerated for a time but slapped at and batted away whenever it grew too intense.

By the start of her sophomore year we were each the other's most faithful cell phone companions.

—◻—

Here is part of my report after coming home from the first day of orientation in Yayoi's sophomore year:

Yayoi bitched about my failure to answer my cell when she called, evidently at 1:30 in the morning, about god knows what. Yasuko demonstrated the name of her club "Body and Soul" to me by caressing my chest (body) and my head (soul). Then she scampered off. Rikako thrice plucked hairs out of my beard and once patted me on the ass. Yes, it's springtime in Nangaku.

April 2003

That spring, Yayoi joined a noncredit TOEFL class, perhaps in the naïve belief that being my student again would impede my ability to sexualize her, though it was hard for a man of my generation to read that intention in the uplifting foundation garments and low-cut tops that she seemed to favor every Wednesday.

In any event, she stopped attending in mid-semester and indeed, dropped out of the picture altogether until shortly before I was to depart for the Great Satan on vacation in August.

Yayoi Shimamura is in heat again.

She initiated a text-messaging spree last night that gradually escalated into... Well, let me copy these down.

She told me her new phone-mail address.

I thanked her and told her that I would look forward to seeing her after my return, if I am not arrested. Then...

Yayoi: *Really? I could understand. Ha-ha-ha. Will you back to America? I surprised at the news. We will go Los angeles and San Francisco an week later! If you will be America, we shall go shopping together in Rodeo Drive. I would like to go Hurry Winston!!*

I hinted that I just might have treated her to something on Rodeo Drive if she had stuck with the TOEFL class.*

---

* I will direct-quote only Yayoi's half of this torrid exchange and summarize my highly injudicious comments. After all, Yayoi may someday decide to write a memoir of her own with the intention of humiliating me, and I would not want to be accused of having poached all her best material.

Yayoi: *I should have studied harder. Where is your home?*

Me: *Illinois, sooooo far from California. I am drunk now, so I can't talk to a sexy woman. Sorry...*

Yayoi: *Are you OK? I am sooooo ~ pity to talk to cool guy! And you are always strenge... I am now drawing pictures.*

I apologized for indeed being strange, and for being old to boot. I indicated an inability to resist the combination of her bitchy attitude and sexy body, and strongly implied that she was always welcome to visit my apartment.

Yayoi: *You are about to say terrible. Even I have naïve heart... Please don't too drink.*

In my reply, written mostly in Japanese, I aimed for an image of a lonely man who was done drinking for the night, sitting in the glow of the TV in the living room of his apartment—his very much *unlocked* apartment. In retrospect, I can see that I botched the syntax.

Yayoi: *I can't understand your saying a little...you are strenger!! I can't go now, but give you my photo. It is so cute that you may be melty.*

I eagerly opened the allegedly gooey attachment, only to find a picture of some sort of African tribal mask. My final reply consisted in toto of an anguished cry of defeat.

Yayoi: *Good night! Have a sweet dream.* [Cute emoticon]

I went and locked the door after that last exchange. Having cleaned the toilet... for nothing. I knew it was a long shot anyway.

August 2003

—¤—

The vampire paradigm always felt like the best fit to describe my interactions with NU women—specifically, the rule that a bloodsucker must be invited into your home before he can enter and do vampiry stuff.

Oh, sure, he can make goo-goo eyes at his target and murmur at her in a buttery Slavic accent and hover around her doors and windows; but until that young lady says "Step on in and take a load off" or words to that effect, he remains impotent.

The typical NU girl seemed bemused by my murmuring and hovering and had no use for it, but Yayoi was different; like a bored twelve-year-old keeping a soccer ball in the air, she reveled in seeing how long she could keep me hovering.

—¤—

Yayoi Shimamura is safely in the US now, so there is no chance of getting into mischief.

August 2003

Yayoi must be back from her trip to the US by now, but has chosen not to pick up our game of telephone tag again.

September 2003

Yayoi Shimamura...called Saturday night just as I had gone to bed. I called back and yakked for over an hour.

She hinted that she wanted to go see Pirates of the Caribbean *on Sunday, but I backed off on that one. I was limping toward payday...*

September 2003

I should have been out on a date with Yayoi right now, but she cancelled late last night due to a zemi thing.*

September 2003

Then came the 2003 Christmas party at my apartment, with all the usual suspects.

Nanako got drunk, bitched about her boyfriend and his new "sex friend," and loudly proclaimed that she doesn't like sex. I gave her prescription antidepressants and the boys gave her a huge glass of straight gin. Kohei vomited repeatedly in the toilet and then cleaned it neater than it had been before. Ken-chan and Jiro bitched about Plotz† and pestered me for porn until I lent them a blow-job video. I also introduced them to the "Hot or Not" website and, while I was at it, the nude celebrity website, too.

Then, after many rumors, Yayoi finally showed up around 10 or so. She looked gorgeous, but claimed she has a boyfriend. She took over my seat next to the computer. When I confessed to being as old as [prominent comedian] *Joji Tokoro, she promptly got on the Net and looked up Joji's bio.*

Before I knew it, it was 1 a.m. I have no idea how noisy we were or how annoyed the neighbors would have a right to be. I did occasionally caution the lads (and Yayoi), and stopped the music and never turned on the TV. But still, I feel awful about it. I'm surprised the landlady hasn't rung me up today. (Maybe it's because I've kept the phone off the hook much of the day.)

I suppose at some point in time, it will be one of those parties that pass into legend. But in its immediate aftermath, I just feel sleazy, cheap…and old.

December 2003

The photographic record does not bear out such a gloomy postmortem. There is a wonderful shot of a very delighted me having faux anal intercourse with a shirtless Jiro, who sports a very

---

* I.e., an event related to her research seminar.

† Rotund successor to me as their second-year English teacher

convincing grimace. And an even more memorable one of the drunken Nanako pinning me to the floor in a full-body hug.[*]

Perhaps I felt down partly because this party had finally breached the Indecent Exposure barrier, with me whipping it out in front of Jiro and Ken-chan. But no, that would be a cause for depression in them, not me.

No way around it, my sour mood was surely a product of Yayoi having discovered my age. Surely, she would no longer require the hovering services of a forty-seven-year-old.

— ¤ —

A party on Wednesday snapped me out of it a little. In a reversal of the Christmas party, Toru got outrageously drunk and couldn't walk to the station, while Nanako remained lucent. I flirted with Cow-Island Girl and asked Rikako if a man's size was important. Kayo Mitani asked me for advice on good kissing, and I told her not to bring the tongue into play too early. It was good therapy. Upon our breaking up, I calmly told Nanako that I would go home and have sex by myself. I suppose I probably did.

January 2004

And so another school year wound down with my chances re Yayoi dwindling away to nothingness. Surely, the thing was a dead letter. At the end of the day, a college girl either wants to jerk off a creepy-looking, married, bald foreigner 2.47 times her age while he slaps her naked titties around, or she doesn't. There oughtn't to be any middle ground on that sort of thing.

Then again, springtime at NU always brought a potent sense of renewal.

---

[*] I look terrified in the photo and for good reason. Experience had taught me by then that the relationship between an NU girl's passion and the NU girl herself was analogous to that of toothpaste and tubes, re the whole issue of re-containment. However, this episode would prove to be the apex of Nanako-Muggins relations.

Chicks are likewise boosting my ego. Yayoi is saying again that she wants to be taken out to dinner. I've been putting that off for some reason that I cannot fathom. Yesterday morning, Wakako Endo checked in, saying she wants to get together soon. I got out old pictures of her and masturbated furiously, twice.

May 2004

Several months of my ever-dwindling life expectancy later...

I contacted Yayoi Shimamura over the weekend about going out for dinner, which she had proposed months earlier. She was at Hiroshima for the [atom bomb memorial] ceremony at the time. We messaged back and forth but in the end I decided it was too much trouble to work out a time and cancelled, probably pissing her off for good.

August 2004

—◻—

The years were tumbling by, and many of Yayoi's peers, having upped their TOEFL scores in my classes, were leaving to study abroad for a year...and then coming back—changed, changed utterly.

I went shopping in the morning and met Yasuko Hirata in Uni supermarket, just back from a year in Canada. I kissed her right there amidst the meats.

March 2005

Yayoi's arc, meanwhile, remained devoid of any such burnishing adventure. Finally, by the summer of 2005—the middle of Yayoi et al's senior year, I decided that the prospects for an illicit affair with her truly had evaporated, that it was safe to go back in the water.

Then, just as I thought it was safe to go back in the water, Yayoi Shimamura re-emerges with outrageously flirtatious emails. In the latest one she asserts that her boobs are far prettier than Todd Plotz's.

August 2005

Later that month…

Yayoi cooled her jets so I had no feminine distractions, apart from porn.

That autumn I turned fifty years old and very much felt it, in no small part due to the dizzying off-and-on flirtations of Yayoi.

Graduation for the 2002 entering class was today. As usual, timing was a problem. I rushed over to the chapel during lunch break from my intensive class…and finally had about 10 minutes to take pictures with the two Mamikos, Ayako, Cow-Island Girl, my old butt-fucking pal Jiro, Kiko Kogawa, Kayo Mitani, etc. I failed to find Yayoi Shimamura and other luminaries. Then I fled back by bicycle to finish the class, my head already throbbing with pain.

March 2006

And so Yayoi had graduated and was out of my life once and for all. Then, later that month:

Yayoi Shimamura emailed to say she wants to get together for coffee. I have not responded yet.

Some small part of me still hovers to this day.

41

Just Lean Back
and Enjoy It

First you will come to the Sirens who enchant all who come near them. If any one unwarily draws in too close and hears the singing of the Sirens, his wife and children will never welcome him home again, for they sit in a green field and warble him to death with the sweetness of their song.

– The Odyssey

It was a vivacious Marxist at D University who first wrapped me around her little finger—or rather, wrapped her little finger around part of me.

"Har! Har! How ya doin'?" Shizue would snarl after sneaking up behind me at the campus bus stop and tickling my ribs. She was a little teapot, short and stout, with rusty Orphan Annie curls. I never had her in a class but befriended her through her club, the DU English Speaking Society, whose noontime meetings I was easily lured to.

DU was my first university job in Japan. Every Tuesday and Thursday morning I would propel myself from bed before dawn, slap on a boxy blue suit and a tie and my enormous Eighties-appropriate glasses, and cram myself into a diagonal Twister position on a rush-hour train packed with mocking schoolgirls.

The university was famous for its radical leftist slant. I cared not that the students might possess collectivist views, but it bothered me a great deal that they mostly possessed testes, and that they were dour and uncommunicative. Thus, attendance of the "noon activity" with the English Speaking Society, while unpaid, restored my faith in human nature, featuring, as it did, a chance to play English games and enjoy idle chitchat in a lecture hall with volatile and testes-free personages like Shizue.

—◻—

The pivotal moment of my career took place during one such noontime gathering.

The club president began the meeting with several announcements which, as per club rules, he set about delivering entirely in English, so that no one, myself included, had any idea what he was saying. Like me, he wore a suit, the better to remind the minions that he was club president. He strode to the lectern and began to hack his way through his checklist, merrily butchering tenses and disemboweling vowels along the way.

I wedged myself into one of the fold-down seats amid the geeky ESS members. The Kremlinesque suit—"grownup costume" was my preferred term—was not a fashion that I ever grew comfortable with. My uniform in later years would consist of khakis, a blue open-collar dress shirt (polo shirts in warmer weather) and sneakers. Just starting out as a university teacher, I believed that a suit and tie would make it harder to unmask me as a fraud.

I still had hair in those days, too. To be sure, a perfectly round beanie of bare flesh on my crown had begun its inexorable march to join forces with my expanding forehead, but for the time being I had that crop-circle confined to a three-inch diameter and tried to forget about it.

And so the president droned on. Shizue, sitting directly behind me, lost the battle of attention early on. Having no mobile phone to turn to (it being the Eighties), she became mesmerized by my bald spot—by a roundness so perfect that it ought not to be found in nature—and absent-mindedly sent out a finger to languidly trace the perimeter of the thing.

Upon sensing this intrusion, I tensed. It occurred to me that I could have brushed her hand away, perhaps throwing in a dirty look—the professional, dignified response—in which case I am certain that my entire subsequent teaching career would have veered onto a much more conventional and joyless path. Instead, I leaned back to grant her easier access to my scalp. Shizue giggled and dug in.

—◻—

N University's International Relations Department has emerged as the type of place where I could be quite content to grow older and balder and one day pitch forward on my lectern spitting up blood and dying. I like it that much so far, anyway.

April 1990

This, after teaching part-time at NU for all of three weeks. Specifics would follow:

It's got a beautiful campus, fairly modern facilities, and classes that consist about 50% of incredibly beautiful young women. And they want to speak English. And they try.

And my Friday classes are loaded enough with young wenches that I actually look forward to waking up at 6:20.*

June 1990

—◻—

The commute to NU's Yokohama Campus from central Tokyo, where I lived with Mrs. Muggins in those days, was just as grueling as the commute to DU, and yet fatigue simply melted away as the Nangaku campus hove into view.

---

* In defense of that "wenches" remark, I was on a Shakespeare kick at the time—had recently seen Kenneth Branaugh and Emma Thompson do *Lear* at the Tokyo Globe, in fact. The vocabulary rubs off after a while.

Partly, this was just a function of NU's superior infrastructure. The school offered a faculty shuttle-bus from the nearest train station, whereas getting to DU entailed a crowded public bus that terminated at a new exurban campus composed of severe blond-brick edifices. The mostly treeless and girl-less expanse suggested a low security prison for white-collar criminals.

Arriving at NU was an altogether different experience.

—▫—

I wonder if I'm edging into some sort of midlife crisis. Perhaps I'm destined to try something really dumb that will end in horrible humiliation, like that suffered regularly by Teddy the Sociology professor at Mankato. But the fact is, I spend a lot of time—probably a lot more than is really healthy—imagining what it would feel like to fuck these girls. There are just so darn many of them to imagine doing it with, and so little time.*

June 1991

That faculty microbus chugs its way up a typically precipitous Yokohama hill (Geographically, our city has been described as "San Francisco without the personality") before hitting a dreary, barren plateau dominated by a monolithic Soviet-style condominium. The route then veers to a two-lane, potholed side road that winds its way under a low canopy of deciduous trees, through which blotches of white begin to be glimpsed. These white flashes grow more persistent until you emerge from the mini-forest and find

---

* At Mankato State, my alma mater, Teddy was well liked for reaching out to students, male and female alike, and for showing concern about our futures. He was married, fortyish, and just couldn't stop hanging out in student bars, where, feeling inexplicably at home, he would drink too much and hit on chicks.

One night, my friends found him in the Rathskeller with the trifecta of blood, sweat, and tears exuding from various parts of his head after an unprofitable encounter with an enraged boyfriend. I never saw him after that, nor wanted to. He was a cautionary tale that haunted me during my early NU years.

yourself suddenly and exquisitely *here*, on the mountaintop, deposited smack in the center of a cluster of alabaster temples.

An early morning fog may linger at this altitude, and from this fog might emerge the angelic forms of any number of NU women, each with her own bluebird perched on her shoulder (or so it seems in memory), with a song in her heart and a dog-eared English textbook clutched to her bosom.

You instantly want to rest your knees on the warm red brick paving and give thanks to God almighty for making you a Nangaku English teacher. You feel lighter, airier...ennobled even, just to bask in the presence of these mythical beings. Their smiles radiate some meth-like property that puts a new spring in your step, their singsong morning greetings hit the cortex like so many lines of cocaine. Side effects may include excessive sweating, accelerated heartbeat, high body temperature, blurred vision, insomnia, palpitations, convulsions, irregular heartbeat, obsessive behaviors, paranoia, inflated self-opinion, chest-thumping, divorce, anxiety, agitation, sudden unemployment, destitution, euphoria, compulsive memoir-writing and chronic pantslessness.

And so another day at NU begins.

I had always hoped, over these last ten years, to make new friends, and expected those friends to be like me in age, foreign-ness, and maybe even profession. Instead, the people who seem to be most in tune with me are a bunch of mostly gorgeous 19- and 20-year-old girls. It's taken me a while to accept that this is true. But now I figure...why fight it? So far their gorgeousness hasn't gotten in the way of the friendship. But the last images that flicker through my conscious mind every night before I fall asleep are of any number of them, in deliciously sinful situations. I hope I can retain the distinction between fantasy and reality.

May 1994

—◻—

It was a different Japan in the late Eighties and early Nineties. Blending in was not an option for non-Asians. Caucasians and darker-skinned foreigners were still rare and regarded as curiosities. You could walk quietly down a street wearing a dignified blue business suit and carrying a briefcase, or you could trace the very same path skipping merrily in a bathrobe woven entirely of broccoli and waving a pair of live iguanas over your head, and in either case you would attract approximately the same sort of wary stares from your Japanese hosts.

Many foreigners found this atmosphere stifling and exclusionary and oppressive, and soon bugged out. Some of us chose to find it liberating.

Sweet Music Together

Rory: I love Ronald Reagan! He's a great leader.
Lori: Love Ronald Reagan? Why do you love that wrinkly old rat?
Rory: I love Ronald Reagan's wrists. I'd love to rub his slender wrists.
Lori: You're crazy, Rory. Lie down and relax. Relaaaax…

—Josh Muggins, dialogue for the practice of *l* and *r* pronunciation (1992)

So, here we are sitting around my pseudo-bachelor pad one afternoon in 1994, Kimi and Ruriko and I, when the two girls simultaneously start emitting these odd, escalating, orgasmic caterwauls.

I haven't laid a finger on them, I swear, unless it was to momentarily grab one of their heads to steady myself on the way to the bathroom. My one-room unit, cluttered with a synthesizer and sundry other electronica, is a typical Japanese abode in which life is lived mainly on the floor. So this sort of head-clutching by an elder rising to his feet is sanctioned (I think).

Kimi and Ruriko are sophomores who took my required English class as freshmen. Each is attractive in her own way; indeed, it would be hard to say which of the two has inspired my aging gonads to more astounding feats of spermatogenesis during our eighteen months of acquaintance. I really should start keeping better records. In any event, having them together in my apartment emitting orgasmic noises might seem a thing devoutly to be wished. And yet, I am not happy.

"No, no, no," I mutter as I check the playback through headphones. "It still doesn't sound right. It doesn't sound like *yawning."*

— ☐ —

We are recording a song together, don't you see, one titled "A Philosophy Professor's Lullaby," one of a dozen original tunes that I have composed and arranged for an album of humorous ditties that I hope to release by the end of that very month, in time for the annual school festival at the start of November.

The lyrics, which lose too much in translation from Japanese to English to merit reproduction here, presuppose a philosophy professor thinking aloud as he lulls a room full of students to sleep. I have invited Kimi and Ruriko today to provide the yawns and snores that gradually crescendo in the background as the professor's oration grows ever more numbing.

"The thing is... Oh, you're going to get mad at me for this."

"What? What?"

"Well, the snoring—that's great! No problem at all with the snoring."

True enough. To be sure, Ruriko's snoring is like a long-shoreman sleeping off a bender, almost off-puttingly good.

"But the yawning..."

"What about it?"

"Promise you won't get mad at me?"

But they know me better than that.

"It's just that... Well, it sounds like two women in the throes of sexual pleasure."

"Huh??"

"Whaaat?"

"Only *you* would think that!"

"Bad, Muggins! Bad! *Bad!*"

"See? I told you you'd get mad."

"But you're so *disgusting!*"

"Let's take it from the top."

—▫—

The International Relations Department of NU was established in 1985 and welcomed its first entering class the following year. Its founding professors were earnest, idealistic, mostly brilliant men and women committed to fostering international understanding and world peace.

Early in the planning stage, those professors made the quite astute decision not to depend on NU's prepackaged English language program as administered by the necrotic English Department with its vague and careless curriculum and jaded Japanese instructors.

They opted instead to set up and maintain a spanking new English program of their very own, despite having no language-education specialist among their number. I imagine that the discussion went something like this:

Professor A: We anticipate a student body that will consist overwhelmingly of young Japanese females passionate about improving their English skills.

Professor B: Right. So let's hire a staff of equally passionate native-speaking English teachers, even though the available workforce here in Japan is overwhelmingly male and as lecherous as proboscis monkeys on shore leave.

Professor C: And let's not supervise these teachers very closely once we've hired them. Surely they'll work with that much more dedication if they know we trust their judgment and that no one is looking over their shoulders.

Professor D: Also, let's encourage both our students and those simian native-speaking teachers to interact with each other as much as possible outside the classroom so as to maximize the potential for cultural-linguistic exchange. We certainly don't want them feeling constrained by any sort of "boundaries."

Professor E: Agreed! What could possibly go wrong?

All: Here, here! Pip, pip!

—◻—

People are practically climbing over barbed wire to get into my class. I just finished reading the first batch of delightful written homework, highlighted by that of a preternaturally gorgeous, big-titted babe named Sayuri which said that my smile reminds her of her former Canadian lover. Spring is in the air at Nangaku.

April 1993

From about my third year on, my reputation was curated by former students who sold me wholesale to the incoming generation every spring, so that freshmen were inclined to suppose me some sort of high priest of pedagogy before they had even met me. All I had to do was not blow it.

Similarly, I was inclined to love NU chicks before I had even met them. I had no "type" per se. I liked sophisticated chicks for their sophistication and naïve chicks for their naivety. Regarding body type, I was just as likely to rave in my journal about some skinny "model-like" entity (e.g. Kimi) as I was about a zaftig (e.g. Ruriko). In the end, the thing that bound all the objects of my worship together was simply their ineffable NU-ness.

You could say that the entering class of 1993 had a deep bench. The aforementioned Sayuri was indeed gorgeous and curvaceous and moderately flirtatious, and yet I recall her almost as vaguely now as she no doubt recalls me. There were just too many gorgeous and moderately flirtatious competitors wafting around.

There was Toko, for example, a goofy, long-limbed, big-boned girl prone to a manly, arm-swinging style of walking and ostentatious declarations of love. She took it upon herself to act as my agent, promoting me to all her friends.

On Toko's birthday, I played a Billie Holiday tune on the classroom speakers and ran toward her in slow motion when she took the "kiss" option. What a zany guy! T-shirts bearing my self-portrait are due to appear soon. *

June 1993

Toko's friends included the aforementioned ditzy-but-sweet Kimi, with the cherubic face of an eight-year-old perched atop a lingerie model's body; the Venus-figurine-like, self-possessed Ruriko, acerbic token homely chick Sachiyo, and an unfailingly upbeat, braces-sporting, high-cheekboned woman-child named Sayaka, whom I was allowed to call *Sawayaka*, meaning "refreshing."

Within our first semester together, Toko organized a class barbecue party, a bowling event, and an unusually raucous bar party at which she bombarded me with sexual innuendo. She did, in fact, have t-shirts bearing my likeness produced and tried to force everyone in the class to order one.

And she was just getting warmed up. Had I announced one day in her freshman class that, darn the luck, I had just killed a meddling Congressman and now our whole cult would all have to commit mass suicide, she would have seen to it that everyone chugged their cup of Kool-aid before cheerfully draining her own.

Back in Mortonville, Illinois, the twentieth-year reunion of my high school class was held around the same time as these Toko-inspired events. A card informed me that the reunion would make us all feel "as if we're eighteen again."

I felt so sorry for them. When your workday begins with thirty young Japanese adults eagerly repeating a dialogue about their

---

* The alternative birthday treat to "a kiss from the teacher" was "a piece of gum." In later years, this morphed into "a piece of gum I've had in my pocket for the past four months" to stack the deck. Those opting for the kiss received a peck on the cheek or hand.

desire to rub Ronald Reagan's wrists, you don't crave artificial sources of rejuvenation.

— ¤ —

After class one day, Kimi and Sachiyo approached me from opposite sides and began jabbering at me simultaneously. I cut them both off.

Me: I'm sorry, Sachiyo, but Kimi should go first, because she is prettier.

Kimi promptly resumed giving me her excuse for missing our next class, oblivious to the umbrage spraying forth from Sachiyo like icy water from a defective sprinkler.

— ¤ —

In October, my birthday fell on a class day. I received two cakes, a fruit basket, a life-sized posterboard cut-out of the pop singer Hikaru Nishida cheerfully hawking a cold remedy that someone had swiped from in front of a pharmacy, and a bunny costume, which I was obliged to put on.

Around the same time, Toko organized a lunch-hour English discussion group that was to meet three times a week. In exchange for attending, I received a homemade *bento* lunch.

On average, I would squeeze out at least one good funny per meeting that would summon forth the healing laughter of Nangaku girls, so that in memory the group now endures as my personal Algonquin Round Table, though in reality there were probably no more than forty sessions.

And topics tended not to be particularly elevated. "Why do boys prefer petite girls to big girls?" was one theme introduced, not surprisingly, by Toko.

Toko: All boys in our class like Kondo-san and Sayaka! It isn't fair!

Me: I like you.

Toko: Oh, thank you, Muggins! I *love* you!

Me: But I like Kondo-san and Sawayaka, too.

Toko: Arrrgghh! Why? *Why,* Muggins? *Why*??

Me: [Shrugging] Cute.

Toko: What kind of girls do you like? Small ones?

Kimi: You like big boobs, don't you?

Me: Well, I'm certainly not opposed to them.

Toko: Come on! Who do you like! Tell us!

Me: Hmm... Some of the girls in my class for English majors are pretty good.

Kimi: In what point?

Me: Well, they're small—

Toko: Aaarrrgggbh!

Me: Just kidding.

Kimi: But I think English majors aren't as funny and interesting as we are.

Sachiyo: Yeah, they don't have so much personality. They're like

Barbie dolls.

Toko: They have *no nipples!*

Me: What? Jesus!

Kimi: What do boys want, anyway?

Here, there ensued a lengthy speculative discussion of this question, during which I turned invisible, a superpower I often assumed without effort at conclaves of IR females.

Sawayaka: What do *you* think, Muggins?

Kimi: Oh, yes! Muggins, you are a boy!

Toko: Is he a boy?

Kimi: He's…sort of a boy.

Me: Thank you, Kimi. And nice job using *sort of.*

And thus I found myself the haver or knowledge that Nangaku females did not have but wanted—a rare position for me indeed, despite my being, you know, their teacher and all.

Me: I'm not sure you really want to know what boys want.

Toko: Oh, tell us, Muggins!

Sawayaka: Yes, please tell us!

Me: Well… It's just that… Well, you see…

Sawayaka wasn't going to make this easy for me, sitting there all innocent and eager for knowledge with a sunbeam glinting off her braces. But she wasn't about to let me off the hook, either.

Me: Okay. The thing is, they just want to have sex with you.

Toko: What do you *mean?*

Me: I mean, they just want to have sex with you.

All: ………..

Sachiyo: No, no. It can't be only that.

Kimi: It's too simple.

Toko: Yeah.

Me: Your problem is thinking that male thinking is a complicated as *your* thinking. It isn't. They just want to have sex with you.

Kimi: Yeah, okay. I get that. But really, what do they *want?*

Me: Pretty much, they just want to have sex with you.

Kimi: But isn't it—

Me: They. Just Want to. Have...

Sachiyo: Stop saying they want to have sex with us!

Me: Well, maybe not so much with *you.*

Sachiyo: Hey!

Sawayaka: What about you, Muggins? Is that what *you* want?

Me: Hey, how about those Yokohama Bay Stars?

To this day, "They have no nipples" remains the most efficiently vicious remark I have ever been present to hear any woman say about other women. If, God forbid, I were to find myself entangled in a fantasy sports league, They Have No Nipples is what I would name my team.

—◻—

The Department of International Relations invited Native American activist Dennis Banks for a workshop and series of culture-sharing events that December. I knew nothing about it until emerging from my classroom for lunch and finding, quite contrary to my expectations, a dignified, fifty-something gentleman in aboriginal garb and braided hair sitting at the edge of our quad with an immense drum, which he proceeded to beat.

Toko and her friends, though lowly freshmen, had somehow been placed in charge of this event. Someone had even seen fit to give Toko a megaphone, which sparked gasoline-on-fire metaphors in my mind.

I parked myself on a bench on the outskirts of the activity between two pretty juniors and proceeded to make snarky comments as my freshman friends and a few older students belonging to a seminar on aboriginal groups joined hands and began to move laterally, Hava Nagila-style, to the drumbeat. That's when I first heard the megaphonic banshee cry of *Muhhhh-giiins!*

I tried to cringe back and hide behind my seatmates, but they were the petite type that Toko so despised and thus offered little cover. She kept after me—*Muhhhh-giiins! Muhhhh-giiins! Come on, come ooooon! Muhhhh-giiins, come out here!!* —as relentless and ruthless as white subjugation of the Red Man, until I succumbed, stepped forth, and took her hand.

I became something like the ninth link of a rump chain that looked—and felt—tiny in the vast chasm that was our quad, with gawkers peering and pointing at us not only from every side at ground level, but from upper-floor vantage points all around us as well. *If only a kindly lone gunman would put me out of my misery…* I felt particularly conspicuous being on the end of the chain, not to mention bald and foreign.

But soon enough, my free hand was scooped up by a comely sophomore, and thereafter our chain grew apace, eventually becoming a complete circle that stretched to the boundaries of the quad, absorbing spectators almost as soon as they arrived on the scene.

It dawned on me midway through lunch hour that I knew most of the people in the circle, that not a few of them owned t-shirts bearing my likeness—and that, mayhap, the circle's rapid formation after my joining was no mere coincidence.

Somehow, Toko's fomenting of a Cult of Personality on my behalf had started paying off, to the extent that gyrating spastically around the quad in broad daylight to an alien drumbeat became a cool thing to do the moment that I started doing it. I began to see other foreign English teachers in the mix, too, albeit resentfully, as Toko and her friends led us seamlessly into a series of figure-eights and bridges and other pseudo-square-dance moves.

One has to commit to these sorts of things, as when going to a nudist colony or launching a megachurch, and so I did, gyrating with ever more verve and grinning like an Ecstasy devotee in a paintball fight, while seething menacingly through the Toko-ward side of my mouth:

"I won't forget you for this."

I still haven't forgotten her for that.

—◻—

The break between school years in Japanese universities spans all of February and March. Living, as we were, in a pre-email world, this meant going cold turkey on chick contact.

When I failed to receive any deliveries of chocolate on Valentine's Day, I had to write, seal and post a letter to Toko to complain. Her response was tardy but conciliatory. I tried to keep busy with my new hobby, writing and arranging humorous songs on my Mac Color Classic, always keeping the girlfriends in mind as my target audience.

I met them en masse on Sophomore Orientation Day early in April, a chance encounter in the first-floor lounge of the International Relations building, and there was much rejoicing. Sawayaka had grown so radiant in the intervening months that I feared turning to stone if I looked straight at her for too long. She looked as if she had aged from twelve to sixteen. In another year or so, I marveled, she could be added to the fantasy registry.

Sensing that my interest was drifting elsewhere, Toko hugged me right there by the seminar lockers and induced me to kiss her on the forehead in front of her male peers. Then I invited her and her friends over to discuss cooperation on my album project, taking their assent for granted.

—▢—

To enter NU and become a "Nangaku Woman"™ is to become part of a brand—a brand defined not by a formidable natural beauty so much as by a certain poise and confidence, often manifested as a signature springy stride bordering on a feminine swagger. It is to become heir to a unique and specific sense of fashion; it entails mastery of certain cosmetic and foundation garment technologies that forever lay beyond my ken.

Ruriko was a case in point. She lives in my memory as the saliva-inducing completed project that she became by the end of her sophomore year. It is somewhat jarring to review my earliest photographs of her, fresh out of high school, during a spring semester in which she lurked shyly and inconspicuously in the shadow of her more flamboyant friends, Toko and Kimi. Her freshman ID photo suggests a puppy that has just been kicked without cause.

In early October 1993, a few weeks into her second semester, I eyed her in the front row.

"You look different," I said.

"Oh? Do I?"*

"What *is* it, Ruriko? What's changed?"

"I'm sure I don't know," she said, but she knew. Oh, she knew.

The students were paired off for various speaking and pronunciation exercises while I circulated, offering tips and vocabulary. Whenever I passed Ruriko's desk, I would revive my theme of the day.

"I can't quite put my finger on it, but you changed something. Your hair is the same, right?"

"Um, pretty much."

The constant attention was beginning to rattle her: *He's going to figure it out... And when he gets it, he's going to blurt it out for everyone to*

---

* If the banter between N. University denizens and me sometimes comes off as polished and shticky to the point where the reader may well wonder why on earth these smoothly communicating young women are subjected to English classes in the first place, there is an explanation for that.

In fact, most of our real-life interaction involved switching back and forth between languages, with one of the participants always groping for unfamiliar words. It's what we in the language ed trade call "negotiation of meaning," and in its raw form, it is not pretty. In real life, the exchange above probably went something like this:

Me: You look different.
Ruriko: Different? *Chigaimasu?*
Me: You are different, somehow. *Dokoka de.* I mean, your appearance.
Ruriko: Ap-peer...?
Me: The way you look, I mean. It's different.
Ruriko: Eh??
Me: Kao to ka, nanka kawatta desho.
Ruriko: Ah, so?

Thus, my policy has been to spare readers the agony of these negotiations by boiling things down. Lord knows, you suffer enough reading my books.

hear… And there's nothing I can do to stop him.

Later, I blurted out, "Oh, it's your eyebrows! What did you do? You thinned them out, didn't you?" in front of the whole class and Jesus and Buddha and Uatu, the Marvel Comics Watcher.

It could have been worse. I could have mentioned the push-up bra.

— ☐ —

It's hard to pinpoint when it happened, but at some point my affection for this whole bunch vaulted all the way past friendship into a very simple and honest love.

May 1994

I got two tickets to the NU orchestra's concert; I took Toko. I wanted to see the NU drama group's new play; I took Sawayaka. If I suffered from a four-hour erection after sitting next to Sawayaka, well, Sachiyo was handy to kill the darned thing off. Each member had her role.

On my Mac, I had input two sounds that I could substitute for the default beep: Sawayaka's delightful singsong "Hallow? Hallow? This is Sayaka!" and Toko's histrionic "Please *make love* me!" I generally went with the former.

— ☐ —

In 1994, retirement worries and enfeebled parents and all the other icky crud of middle age still failed to cling to me. For the most part, life chugged merrily along. I had little contact with faculty colleagues or superiors and abundant daily contact with eager, hot young friends.

The only downside was school vacations. Why, oh why, did we have to have vacations?

When my thoughts roam freely—be they lustful thoughts or any other kind—they inevitably drift toward Sawayaka and Toko and all my other NU gyaru-friends. I do love them all so, in my pathetically hopeless middle-aged-man way. It hurts not to see them, not even to talk to them.

September 1994

—◻—

Early that fall, I assembled Toko, Ruriko, and Sawayaka one steamy Sunday afternoon for our virgin recording session. My journal reports that the girls were "blown away" by the new arrangements of the tunes.

But when it came time to lay down the live vocal track, it appears I succumbed to "one of my tension attacks." I was convinced that everyone should stand up while recording, because people are always standing up in recording studios in all the biopics of famous junkie musicians. Had it been only Toko and Ruriko, perhaps I could have muddled through. It was the dazzling presence of Sawayaka, with that persistent beam of sunlight gleaming off her braces, that left me weak at the knees.

Somehow we ground out a stirring recording of "New Nangaku School Song," the chorus of which translated as:

We are the people of Nangaku!
And we aren't all that ashamed to admit it!
Sure, we all wanted to go to Jochi instead,
But we screwed up, so here we are.

—◻—

Ruriko has emerged as the MVP on this project so far—the only singer to show up for every song. I noticed her remarkable sensuality for the first time and whiled away many happy hours wondering how it would feel to hold her hefty, pendular breasts in my hands.

October 1994

Certainly the theretofore laconic Ruriko had come alive during the pivotal weeks of album production. For the first time in our eighteen months of acquaintance, I found out what her laugh sounded like (the Burgess Meredith rendition of Batman's nemesis the Penguin), but I suspect her rocketing to the top of the Fantasy Hit Parade had more to do with the announcement (gleefully made by Ruriko herself) that Toko had finally trapped herself a boyfriend.

I wasn't all that surprised. Toko had aggressively slimmed herself down over the summer, finally concluding that if she couldn't beat the Petite Mafia, she would have to join them. Her paramour was a tanned, strapping, car- and hair-having lad named Hiroki with whom I could not hope to compete. I took the news badly.

—◻—

By the end of the three-day NU school festival in early November, we had moved over one hundred eighty cassette tapes and amassed over seventy thousand yen (seven hundred Yankee dollars) for charity.

Every day, a backing vocalist or two accompanied me around campus, bearing my poster as we pushed our way through the crowds. Not surprisingly, Toko proved to be the most forceful promoter as she tirelessly screeched *"It's Muggins's Debut Albuuuuuum!"* at a dumbfounded multitude.

A great many potential customers were themselves moving among the throng to push their own products on behalf of their clubs or organizations, so we often got bogged down in negotiation: You buy mine and I'll buy yours.

The students generally sold snacks in the one hundred fifty yen range while the album went for six hundred, so such deals were agreeable to me. The only problem was the accumulation of so-called "food" items that simply could not be eaten. One delicacy, octopus balls, usually turned out to be dollops of under-fried dough devoid of any part of an octopus. The worst concoction and also the most ubiquitous was a jiggly Chinese jelly called *anmin-dofu*. A vile enough foodstuff when prepared by professionals, its college festival version suggested microwaved Styrofoam.

On the second day, I hired the luckless Sachiyo as Designated Eater, obliged to make the rounds with me and devour every slimy substance that I had to buy to seal a sale. She seemed happy enough with this arrangement at first, but staged a walkout halfway through her fifth *anmin dofu*.

—□—

My relationships with each of my babe-friends, and with Toko in particular, continue to get more complex, at least in my own mind… Letting a friendship with one of these girls turn physical would mean risking everything I hold dear in the world. And yet, if the chance actually arose, I believe I would jump at it—and God have mercy on my soul.

Anyway, I don't really devote any serious worry-time to the prospect that the above might actually happen. What I do fear is that they will simply drift away from me. Toko's boyfriend represents to me a further dilution of the already very limited time that we still have together. They just don't understand how short our time is.

October 1994

This whine-fest was composed just after my birthday, which was roundly ignored by the group. The freshmen, God bless them, took up some of the slack. Two girls presented me with slices of cake from the on-campus café while a third dropped a whole homemade fruitcake on me, a thing best measured in terms of

---

* And there it is in a nutshell, eh wot? Whether its student-and-teacher, parent-and-child, priest-and-altar-boy, whatever the relationship, it all comes down to *time*. Money—you can always make more of that rubbish. Sperm—same deal. Time is the one truly nonrenewable resource.

Okay, end of philosophical rumination. Back to irresponsible drivel.

pressure per square inch and half-life.

The baker, one Chieko, is noted in my journal mainly for her physical attributes, though I scarcely remember her or them. I gather that she exhibited the kind of body that in another culture might inspire no end of comparisons to outdoor lavatories constructed of brick.

As for her fruitcake, it only reinforced an already unshakable theory of mine that a Japanese girl possesses baking skills in inverse proportion to her hotness.

It was a noxious thing, this fruitcake, like a million *anmin dofu*s compressed into a single tin, and yet I did my best that long, lonely birthday weekend to gnaw my way through it, as if access to an escape route from Shawshank Prison lay on its opposite side.

There were few life-guiding principles that I could claim to cling faithfully to in those days, but among them was this nugget: When a huge-titted freshman girl bakes you a cake, you make your best effort to eat it with a smile.

—◻—

As the days grew shorter toward the end of 1994, the coolness of my once enthusiastic sophomore friends became a pill almost as bitter to swallow as that fruitcake. In theory, we still had noon-hour discussion time during which I was to be presented with a free lunch. The custom had survived the first semester more or less intact, but in the fall, cancellations became ever more frequent until they ceased bothering to inform me and just stopped showing up.

My journal makes numerous references to cards and letters that I sent out in the hopes of "patching things up," though it is unclear exactly what I was attempting to patch up. I had done nothing to give offense. Well, other than nearly two years of nonstop sexual innuendo and leering and embarrassingly public eyebrow-related remarks and insulting critiques of their yawning. But nothing *new*.

—◻—

[Toko and I] *had dinner and coffee in Shibuya, a total of six glorious hours together. We talked about how Hiroki bores her, her future, the dork who writes the self-important humor pieces in her committee's newsletter, why girls are so keen to have boyfriends even though they don't have primitive urges, and more embarrassing misadventures of my Mankato days. I had a ball.*

March 1995

A month earlier I had received a special delivery of Valentine chocolates from Kimi, along with a card bearing a lipstick imprint. But a year or so later, I was hearing that she had quit school to join a theater company, where she was swapping bacteria regularly with a mentor who was older than me. That hurt. Older than me…

Meanwhile, Toko and Ruriko became "Asada Girls," joining the two-year research seminar of a flamboyant faculty lothario who took his students on an annual three-week study tour of Southeast Asian countries. Later that year they badgered me into editing the lengthy English papers they would have to read as part of that excursion, which led to the three of us huddling around a computer screen for hours on end.

They were only using me, of course… But I didn't care about that. It was such a thrill to be around them again, however fleetingly… I was like a junkie getting one last little fix before kicking the stuff once and for all.

December 1995

—◻—

The dawn of the Email Era extended the renaissance in communication…

Hi!! Maggins… I was happy. You are Always unchangable(?) You are always young, looking spirit.

68

I am always changeble. This make me upset. People say, {Toko, You change.}

Who am I?

After 4 month, job begins. I don't know what I should.

Merrid, child, husband, I want to challenge all of them.

I am very sad. sad. I don't know why.

I am very happy, this loveletters between you and me.

LOvE.

Toko

...and, to be sure, there would be postgraduate reunion parties well into the new millennium, but the girls' junior year was really the last hurrah.

In Washington, the watchword is, "If you want a friend, get a dog." My building did not permit pets. But like many a disillusioned American pol, I was learning not to invest too much affection in any individual. Learn to compartmentalize, like the Big Dog in the White House. Love "the Nangaku Woman™" in the general, not in the particular. Before you start hearing Goodbye from one generation, start saying Hello (and, when appropriate, *I love you*) to the next one. That was my take-home point.

The first *Toy Story* movie came out that very year, 1995, and the storyline hit home: As young people get older, they start desiring more sophisticated playthings, and can no longer be satisfied with a wide-eyed, scrawny Caucasoid thing-a-majig that just goofily flaps its limbs and says predictably silly things when its string is pulled.

In the end, I was no match for boyfriends and actual college professors and other such Buzz Lightyears, not to mention the Real World delights that lay beyond graduation.

Fun in the Clinton Years

A man who moralizes is usually a hypocrite, and a woman who moralizes is usually plain.

—Oscar Wilde

<u>June 1995</u>: The office of Chief of Staff Leon Panetta welcomed Monica Lewinsky, 21, as a new unpaid intern.

The line between healthy fantasy and potentially very unhealthy reality is getting fuzzy again. I suppose it's part residual mid-life crisis, spurred on by the fact that some girls seem uncommonly...possible. The leading candidate is a girl named Suzu in my writing class...

Also moving up on the same Hit Parade is a girl named Akiko, who I met in TOEFL class last spring and is now in my Tuesday sophomores class. She's thoroughly, intensely feminine and naive, and has one of those hefty, slightly over-padded bodies that drive me wild—sort of a Ruriko without the attitude.

July 1995

Plagued by body issues in his formative years, young Bill Clinton was no babe magnet. Not until well into adulthood, after he had achieved professional success—and had found and married an understanding soulmate—did he begin to attract female admirers.

Both the number of such admirers and their fervor would increase as his career advanced, and yet Clinton resisted the temptation to cross the line between healthy fantasy and dangerous action perhaps 84.7 percent of the time. For this, I regard him as our greatest president.

Meanwhile, at NU, every day felt like a Million Monica March. So many female admirers, many with those hefty, slightly over-padded bodies that drove me wild, others with the dorky, beanpole bodies or brawny, athletic bodies that also drove me wild—it would probably be quicker just to enumerate the few Japanese-chick body-types that failed to drive me wild—now sending me their English journals via this consarned "E-mail" contraption so that they could be forever captured in cyber-amber for review in my old age.*

—◻—

November 1995: They agreed to meet a few minutes later in Mr. Stephanopoulos' office. There, they began kissing. Ms. Lewinsky unbuttoned her jacket after which her bra was removed, allowing the President to fondle her breasts with his hands and mouth. According to her testimony: "I believe he took a phone call...and so we moved from the

---

* Or for padding a memoir, whichever came first.

Early in the email era, I liked to sign my correspondence to female students "The Sexiest White Man on Campus" and would insist on being addressed the same way. Nangaku women, normally meticulous about English spelling, seemed to struggle with the appellation, as I received a number of emails that began, "Hello, sexist white man on campus."

hallway into the back office... [H]e put his hand
down my pants and stimulated me manually in the
genital area." Ms. Lewinsky then performed
fellatio on the President as he continued to talk
on the phone to a party that Ms. Lewinsky believed
to be a member of Congress.

A big change in my lifestyle this year has come from the double whammy of going on line and getting a fax machine. I seem to acquire a few new E-mail chums every month now, although many of them are people that I meet routinely at school. Still, it's nice to come home and, more often than not, find some cheerful communication from the outside world waiting for me. Today, for example, I read freshman Ichiro Takahara's appraisal of who the hottest babes are in our class, and sent him back my viewpoint.

November 1995

—□—

December 1995: Believing that the President had
forgotten her name during the intervening six-week
period, as he had called her "Kiddo" when they met
in the hallway, Ms. Lewinsky re-introduced
herself. The President insisted that he knew her
name but had lost her phone number, and had tried
in vain to find her in the phone book. They then
moved into the study for their third sexual
encounter.

Emi Denda came over this past Saturday, but she brought a kinda drippy friend along that I'd never met before so it was a bit tedious. I kept having to repress a strange impulse to fondle Emi's breasts with my feet...

December 1995

73

I had come to know Emi, an English major and future teacher, through non-credit intensive courses. She had naturally long eyelashes and thin eyebrows. She grew her brown hair long and sometimes wore it in a single thick braid that she draped over her shoulder so that it dangled down her chest, giving her a frontierswoman vibe; in an parallel universe, she could have been a schoolmarm who drove Pa Ingalls to demon rum and fornication.

She played trombone in the Jazz Club, and I never missed an opportunity to see her perform at school festivals. There was something about watching her blow on an instrument while sliding her hand rapidly back and forth. I brought roses for her that year, so meaningful to me were her sensual glissandos.

—◻—

And then, of course, there's Aki Mino, who, not to be outdone, actually sat on my lap and swiveled back and forth with me as I perused her first draft [of her study-abroad application essay] *and freshmen scattered around the language lab watched in slack-jawed astonishment.*

December 1995

January 1996: The President then cut her off in mid-sentence with a kiss. The ensuing encounter was interrupted when someone came into the Oval Office. According to Ms. Lewinsky, "He zipped up real quickly and went out and came back in... I just remember laughing because he had walked out there and he was visibly aroused..."

—◻—

E-mail buddy Numabe came over with a couple of chicks, Yumiko and Chitose, to help me record new class material—and of course, shave my head.

Numabe gave me software to get on the Internet and we fooled around with that for an hour or so.

February 1996

My dial-up server in those days offered email and message boards only, sans the ability to view the mythical "world-wide web" with a "browser." Numabe brought me Netscape via zip file, allowing the girls and me our first glimpse of the ballyhooed cyberworld through his server.

A preternaturally placid and mature geek, Numabe patiently explained the workings of the "search engine" Lycos. "We can look for a famous actor or singer. Who do you like?"

"Tom Cruise!" burbled Yumiko.

"Sure. If I type Tom Cruise in here and click Go…"

And lo, a Tom Cruise fanpage appeared unto us in a flame of fire out of the midst of the Mac screen, and the screen burned with fire, and the screen was not consumed. That is to say, mosaic blotches slowly resolved themselves into crisp, grinning images of that beloved posterboy for heterosexuality.

It was as Numabe was clicking from one fan page to the next that I heard someone say…

Enough of this crap. Let's look for naked people.

…in an oddly quavering voice that I soon recognized as my own. Numabe dutifully typed "naked people" into good old Lycos and soon had a promising list, from which I made a selection.

The link opened an image that filled the tiny screen of my Mac Color Classic, around which the four of us, on hands and knees, had formed a tight circle. The fleshy mishmash of cubes slowly tightened to smaller cubes, and then smaller cubes still. Caucasian flesh-tone remained the dominant color, though other, more disturbing hues fought to express themselves near the center as resolution increased. *O brave new world, that has such cubes in't!*

Numabe remained impassive; the two girls remained perplexed; only I seemed to grasp where this was heading, and it was not a place one wished to go with two young ladies of new acquaintance.

"Numabe," I stammered, like a Starfleet captain unworthy of command, "get us out of here!" Numabe froze, his eyes slowly widening, before getting a grip and finding Exit.

—◻—

March 1996: "He focused on me pretty exclusively," said Ms. Lewinsky, adding that the President kissed her bare breasts and fondled her genitals. The President then pushed a cigar into her vagina, removed it, and put it in his mouth. "It tastes good," he noted.

I'm having a ball. I got a letter from Suzu Iwasawa the other day on behalf of the senior class, inviting me to their graduation party. I declined, but still... Just when I think, "This is the peak. My NU life can't get any richer or more rewarding than it already is," something happens to prove me wrong. I thank God once again for making me a Nangaku English teacher.

March 1996

April 1996: Ms. Lewinsky was transferred to a new position as an assistant to Pentagon spokesman Ken Bacon. Deputy White House Chief of Staff Evelyn Lieberman cited inappropriate and immature behavior as the reason for the transfer. A career government worker named Linda Tripp then befriended the newcomer at the Pentagon.

Ah, for those zany days before the onset of madness [the start of spring semester]. *Those days of wandering around campus, greeting old friends, ... skipping out on freshman guidance to record the achingly gorgeous duet "Nangaku Waltz" with Yuriko...getting my head shaved by whole squadrons of hot babes...hanging out in the Mac lab with Satchan Fukazawa... getting kissed and hugged by* [English Speaking Club] *president Kaho Takino at Amataro...*

April 1996

—◻—

Summer 1996: Early in the morning of July 19, the day of his departure for the Atlanta Olympics, Ms. Lewinsky received a phone call from the President which led to phone sex. "What a way to start a day," he said after the act was completed. Ms. Lewinsky cited May 21, July 5 or 6, Oct. 22, and Dec. 2 as other occasions of phone sex with the President in 1996.

I'm perfectly aware of how absurd the concept of sex between me and a young woman is, given my age and creeping rotundity. I've been careful not to let my thoughts spill over into words or deeds that could come back to haunt me. It's hard sometimes, though. The Emi Dendas, the Mihoko Kanos, the Yukiko Takahashis, they're just so damn sweet and cute and ripe...and sometimes so seemingly available. * In [a sophomore] class, a girl named Yuki Sawada regularly sits in front, leaning forward and spilling forth such abundant bosoms that I often feel a compulsion to stick a thousand-yen-bill between them at the end of the lesson...*

June 1996

---

* In retrospect, I wish I had not been so keen to use the word *ripe* in describing NU women. Why only that word out of all my unseemly modifiers should discomfit me now, I cannot say. But there it is.

Summer 1996: At the Pentagon, Ms. Lewinsky began
to confide in coworker Linda Tripp about her
relationship with the President.

—☐—

My life makes a difference in the lives of those around me. I do believe it.

June 1996

My second album dropped at the school festival in early November, just days before President Clinton clobbered a hapless Bob Dole to secure himself a second term. Jolly good for him, but the album got decidedly mixed reviews. "Too weird," was a common criticism.*

I was crushed. In my turn as leader of the noon chapel service on campus that month, I spoke about bravely going on in the face of adversity, using the negative comments about my album as an example.†

—☐—

With the President's secretary, Betty Currie,
facilitating, the President and Ms. Lewinsky began
meeting for sex again in 1997, with the
presidential campaign over.

---

* In my defense, the promotional poster clearly stated "11 great songs! Plenty of vomiting!" and "You'll laugh! You'll cry! You'll want to throw up!"

† No, seriously. That's what I talked about.

In her testimony, Ms. Currie acknowledged a
suspicion that the relationship between the
President and Ms. Lewinsky was inappropriate, but
insisted that she consciously avoided learning any
details. When Ms. Lewinsky said, of one encounter,
"As long as no one saw us — and no one did — then
nothing happened," Ms. Currie answered, "Don't
want to hear it. Don't say any more. I don't want
to hear any more."

After class, Honami and I engaged in a totally hypothetical discussion of how much money it would take to get her to engage in "enjo kosai."

January 1997

As the others filed out of the room on that last day of class, I inquired into Honami's spring vacation travel plans.

She was a powerful, jovial junior, a captain of the women's lacrosse squad, our school's only competitive team. She had sharp, smallish eyes and seemed to retain some of her summer training tan even in January. In summers she would achieve a rich, nougaty brownness, inspiring me every year to jabber at her in a faux tribal language under the pretense of mistaking her for a foreign student from Africa, a gag every bit as perennially unsuccessful as it was racist.

"Spring? Only working," she answered, with a sad head-shake. "I'd love to go somewhere, but I just don't have any money."

"Well, that sucks."

"Yeah... Yeah, I suppose I might have to do *enjo kosai*, or something."

Enjo kosai: literally "companionship with support" but more frequently translated by the English media as "compensated dating." It was a new phenomenon at the time and thus still ill-defined, but most considered it a euphemism for a thriving form of call girl activity embraced by some young Japanese women and high school girls.

There was no small amount of hand-wringing over this supposed epidemic, in part because the practitioners tended to be of the comfortable middle-class, and cold-bloodedly cited a desire for such items as designer handbags as their motive; but then again, the wringing of hands over the decadence of today's youth has always been a sort of a national pastime for the Japanese.

Honami's comment hung in the air for several pregnant seconds, during which the room seemed to grow more humid. She had spent a year in the Satan as a high school exchange student and thus knew how to wield the English language with irony. Was she being ironic now? Her tone suggested a genuine sadness and resignation.

"Seriously?" I asked. "You...you would really consider doing something like that?"

"Well...yeah, I guess so," she said, tucking books into her non-designer bag. "I mean, I guess it doesn't hurt anything."

"Hmm, well, I suppose you're old enough to make these sorts of decisions."

"Yeah."

She slung the book bag over her well-marbled shoulder. Had the central heating been turned up at the end of the period? Or was the warmth I was experiencing something internal?

The essential ingredients for *enjo kosai*, as I understood it, were a young woman craving disposable income and a lonely middle-aged man. *I* was a lonely middle-aged man. And now, a young woman in my presence was speaking of cash-flow problems and injecting *enjo kosai* into our conversation. Coincidence? Or destiny?

"Just—you know, hypothetically speaking," I said, swabbing my dried lips furtively with my tongue, "about what would you expect to get for one, er, session...of *enjo kosai*?"

"What? Oh, you mean, money? I hadn't really thought that deeply about it."

"Again, just hypothetically," I burbled.

"Oh, I don't know..."

"Would, ohhh, say, twenty thousand yen be in the ballpark?"

Her eyes fixed on a distant point and she stopped moving.

"Twenty *thousand?* Yeah, sure! I'd do it for twenty thousand!"

"Oh…oh, really?"

"Sure, you bet! Twenty thousand? Gee, I had no idea that guys would pay that much."

"Oh…oh, *really?*"

"For just dinner and boring conversation with someone like me, I mean."

She threw out this comment with a subtle shrug that somehow caused me to flinch, a testament to her athletic musculature. I heard a sputtering sound like someone struggling to start a motor scooter and realized that it was me.

"Wait a second," I said, "wait just a second here. Do you really think that some man is going to pay you twenty thousand yen *just to eat and talk with you?*"

Now it was her turn to rock back on her heels.

"Well…yeah."

"After which he would also *pick up the check,* I suppose?"

"Well…"

Air rushed from my flaring nostrils, producing the sound of a rapidly deflating fantasy. For her part, Honami was numb and confused, "like a duck hit on the head," to employ a Lincolnism.

But this state of defensiveness could not last. Somewhere in the inner machinery of her nimble mind she reminded herself that she was a Nangaku woman. And not merely a Nangaku woman, but an *International Relations* woman, and a *lacrosse* woman. And not merely a lacrosse woman, but a *captain.*

And with every step of recollection, her posture improved until she craned up to her full height, Transformer-like, seeming to tower over me despite my five-centimeter advantage.

"Okay, Muggins, so tell me one thing."

"Yes?"

"Just what did *you* think a man would get from me for twenty thousand yen?"

There was a sudden temperature drop of five degrees

throughout the room. There *was*. I'm sure I didn't imagine it.

—◻—

February 1997: Ms. Lewinsky received a hat pin and
a special edition of Walt Whitman's Leaves of
Grass as late Christmas presents from the
President. A sexual encounter then ensued.

"I wanted to perform oral sex on him...and so I
did. And then...I think he heard something, or he
heard someone in the office. So, we moved into the
bathroom.

"And I continued to perform oral sex and then he
pushed me away, kind of as he always did before he
came, and then I stood up and I said...I care
about you so much; ... I don't understand why you
won't let me...; it's important to me; I mean, it
just doesn't feel complete, it doesn't seem
right."

The President hugged her and said that "he
didn't want to get addicted to me, and he didn't
want me to get addicted to him." They exchanged a
look, after which the President said, "I don't
want to disappoint you," and then allowed Ms.
Lewinsky to perform fellatio until he achieved
orgasm.

Later, Ms. Lewinsky would notice stains on one
hip and on the chest of her navy blue dress. Tests
would confirm that these stains were the
President's semen.

*I got a phone call from the All-Time-Top-Ten-in-the-lusciousness-parade
Naomi Murata, and she was coming on to me. It was so unexpected that I
didn't even pick up on it while I was talking to her. Like a dork, I only
invited her to come to the station to have a donut with me. But after I hung up,
it hit me like the proverbial ton of bricks.*

February 1997

Naomi had graduated a year before without securing stable employment, so the MacGuffin here was "advice about my future." She wanted my help pursuing working holiday packages in English-speaking countries or other options for boosting her job prospects.

She was one of those petite girls that Toko so despised, with Tweety-bird eyes. Since she was also out of school and was the one initiating contact, it seemed unlikely that we could coax a blip from NU's Scandal-o-meter. That is, if she were to insist on performing oral sex on me to completion, or something, in which case I would have been loath to disappoint her.

We had frequent meetings over the next several months, including some in my apartment, but without any sparks. I had been going out quite a bit with Naomi's frenemy Ayana in this same time frame[*] and thus hearing a lot about Naomi's enthusiastic clubbing and man-hunting, which rendered me shy, given my allergy to comparative judgments.

Eventually, I offered her a job as my intern. I needed someone to help me with the Japanese content of the album-promoting, cult-of-personality-fluffing website that I was launching. I suppose "ad hoc assistant" would have been the more accurate term but, things being as they were in those days, *intern* held more cachet.

Naomi has come over twice to assist me with home page matters, and I have given her over 10,000 yen each time. I have not tried anything overt. Discreet hints lead me to believe that she does not feel at all obligated to take off all her clothes and do naked jumping jacks in exchange for this overly generous remuneration… She does, at least, shave my head with lovingly attentive perfectionism. She even did it with the razor last week.

June 1998

It was easy to see why she would inspire a following at clubs

---

[*] As described elsewhere in my oeuvre.

and the envy of Ayana, as she had enormous hooters for such a tiny woman. They were pleasantly squishy in consistency, a datum that I gleaned through the sensors of my scalp and ears during those attentive head-shavings in the close quarters of my kitchen.

And, much as I would like to leave the Naomi story there, I cannot. She never did go abroad for working holiday, nor did she find stable employment as far as I know.

I last heard about her from friends four years later, and the news was not good. She battled a mood disorder that kept her housebound for years, as her employability and lusciousness gradually faded. It is, alas, not an uncommon theme among International Relations alumnae.

<hr>

<u>March 1997</u>: "[T]his was another one of those occasions when I was babbling on about something, and he just kissed me, kind of to shut me up, I think," she said. The President opened her blouse and fondled her breasts through her bra. "He went to go put his hand down my pants, and then I unzipped them because it was easier. And I didn't have any panties on. And so he manually stimulated me." Ms. Lewinsky continued, "I wanted him to touch my genitals with his genitals." The President did so, but did not attempt intercourse. Then Ms. Lewinsky once again performed fellatio on him to completion.

—◻—

Dear Mr. Muggins,

Hi! How are you? I'm busy as always. Well, like you can see, I can write e-mail now. Now I can get in touch with you whenever I want to. Great!

By the way, did I tell you that I finally made it to Berkeley? Well, I did. I finally got an official addmition from Berkeley. And I really happy about it.

Sorry that I didn't inform you earlier, but I hope you are happy for me too.

Before I go any further, I have to thank you again for all your support and everything. I really appreciate it. I would not have made it without you or your classes. I feel very lucky that I had you as my teacher. You are one of the greatest (and the most funniest) teacher I've ever met. I really mean it. I'm not exaggerating! It's my true feeling If I had not taken the TOEFL class last spring, and not had met you, I swear I wouldn't be going to Berkeley. YOU, have changed my life. Anyway, thank you sooooo much ! from all my heart.

Always,
Mai

—¤—

July 1997: President Clinton was "the most affectionate with me he'd ever been" on that occasion, Ms. Lewinsky testified. He caressed her arm, kissed her neck, and spoke highly of her appearance and intelligence. "He remarked...that he wished he had more time for me. And so I said, well, maybe you will have more time in three years. And I was...thinking just when he wasn't President, he was going to have more time on his hands. And he said, well, I don't know, I might be alone in three years. And then I said something about us sort of being together. I think I kind of said, oh, I think we'd be a good team, or something like that. And he...jokingly said, well, what are we going to do when I'm 75 and I have to pee 25 times a day? And... I told him that we'd deal with that..."

Ms. Lewinsky concluded that "I left that day sort of emotionally stunned" because "I just knew he was in love with me."

—◻—

Another day, another IR chick, another intriguing email explaining a series of absences.

...First, I was sickness in these days. It's true. I was sleeping all days with watching TV. Please take care yourself. It's very easy to catch the cold. Especially, nose and cough. As the [pro]verb say that "yamai ha ki kara" This mean is If you are nervous or have some problems, you will be sickness. Actually I was nervous in these days. That is why I got sick.

You must want to know why I was nervous. Maybe you will laugh to hear my story. I had the trouble with my boyfriend. I couldn't understand this problem still now. My boy friend is going abroad for 3 months. It is OK. No problem .But in August the crices happened. A woman called to my mobile phone. She said to me "Do you know I'm his wife ?" I was so shocked to hear that. I didn't know about that. You know it's my first bitter experience. Probably she is real wife, I think. But I can't say any thing until my boy friend coming back to Japan. It is closing the time. Until that time coming, I must stand.

So, at last I was sickness. But as you know, I was lucky I was busy in the summer break. If I didn'T have any business, I can't imagine I was alive or not. I'm sorry to write such a stupid story.

Riko

Later:

Dear Muggins

Thanks for your kindness I feel better. I never think there are many people who feel nervous for the inter-relationships between person and person, woman and man, and so on. I thought I was not the only poor woman.

—◻—

On Monday, I finally corralled Honami Torihata for the first interview in the "Great Nangaku Onna" series, and she did not disappoint, telling about why she hates white men...

At the same time, I'm about as horny as I've ever been in my life. I cruise the Internet looking for nasty images. I dwell on the possibilities I may have with Ayana, with Yuriko...with Emi Denda, who called me last night to come and check her essay at the station. I made a half-hearted attempt to lead her back to my filthy apartment and then maybe try to exchange bodily fluids with her. Instead, I had the privilege of blowing over 2000 yen on her for cake and coffee and a taxi ride to campus, where she had to pick up her trombone.

I got Yuriko's attention by making a huge big deal out of her birthday a few weeks ago (while at the same time neglecting my wedding anniversary). As I told Yuriko myself, I wonder what kind of man I'm becoming... I don't feel guilty about having these feelings, though I do feel a little guilty about that lack of guilt.

On Tuesday, I got Erina Oki and Nina Morishima to shave my head.

June 1997

Careful readers will recall Honami as the lacrosse captain and quasi-*enjo kosai* enthusiast. The Great Nangaku Onna (i.e. "Great Women of NU") interview series, subtitled "The Feature that Exists Solely so that Muggins Can Have Dinner with a Beautiful Woman," would remain a staple of my website for several years.

I hinted at the existence of a secret selection committee that shadowed likely candidates from matriculation until such time that a girl's achievements accumulated sufficiently in her junior or senior year to merit nomination. Only then would she be invited to an upper-middle range ethnic restaurant and compelled to answer questions about her sexual history and weight into a tape recorder, while also getting a chance to publicize the causes dearest to her heart.

Those NU girls—always with the causes.

<u>July 1997</u>: As she was about to leave, Ms. Lewinsky told the President "that I wanted to talk to him about something serious and that while I didn't want to be the one to talk about this with him, I thought it was important he know." She then told him of the <u>Newsweek</u> article then in the works about Kathleen Willey, a former White House volunteer who claimed that the President had sexually harassed her during a private meeting in the Oval Office on Nov. 23, 1993...

The President dismissed the harassment allegation as ludicrous, given that he could have no interest in a small-breasted woman like Ms. Willey.

—▢—

I've had blessedly little to do with Furman these past weeks, though he did horn in on a freshman party on the 20th. I sat next to the amazing Amazoness Wakako Endo most of the evening, and really wanted to see her naked body. But I kept that thought to myself. Furman seemed to think me out of control when I grabbed Satsuki's pigtails and waved them in the air, but I thought it was a relatively subdued evening as such things go.

July 1997

Furman was a senior colleague whom I have described elsewhere as "dwarfish and stealthy," a characterization I stand by.

The party with freshmen was part of my campaign to rehabilitate my image after my live concert at their welcome party that April had devolved into a debacle of equipment failure and alcohol abuse. Satsuki assured me that I was appreciated just for trying, and I instantly fell in love with her, small-breasted woman though she was.

August 1997: Ms. Lewinsky brought birthday
presents for the President, whose birthday is
August 19. "I had set up in his back office, I had
brought an apple square and put a candle and had
put his birthday presents out. And after he came
back in and I sang happy birthday and he got his
presents, I asked him...if we could share a
birthday kiss in honor of our birthdays, because
mine had been just a few weeks before. So, he said
that that was okay and we could kind of bend the
rules that day. And so...we kissed."
  Ms. Lewinsky patted the President's groin area
and indicated her desire to perform fellatio, but
the President did not assent. "He said, I'm trying
not to do this and I'm trying to be good... He got
visibly upset."

Last night...Emi Denda called me and we met at Mister Donut. She gave me wine to thank me for all my help and advice, and more important, let me look at her. Cycling home from that event, I ran into Mana Katsuki on the street and made her pose with me in front of the neighborhood "Warning! Perverts!" sign.

October 1997

Mana co-wrote and directed a movie that was selected for screening by an international amateur film festival in New York. For this and other achievements, she was confirmed as a Great Woman of Nangaku later that year.

—¤—

[On my birthday] *I got a delicious bottle of wine from...Shigeru Kato and ripe-as-a-peach beauty Nami Aoki, the latter of whom I publicly kissed...*
  On Friday, the second period freshmen gave me the individual card

treatment, plus a stocking hat and a cake with a candle. Yu-chan Funada kissed me and I kissed Wakako Endo.

October 1997

<u>Fall 1997</u>: Linda Tripp decided to start taping conversations with Ms. Lewinsky in order to have a record of the details of her affair with the President.

I sometimes wonder if I'm beginning to have a "woman problem"... I wonder if I'm perhaps allowing the wrong aspect of my affection for my pretty young friends to dominate my thinking. (And perhaps too much time spent on the wrong Internet sites has fueled this tendency...) More and more, I have to be careful to edit my E-mailings in order to purge them of innuendo that goes too far—and still I often wonder if, in fact, I've managed to purge all of that.

On the other hand, there's just as much evidence to support the idea that many NU women have a Muggins problem. I kissed two lovely freshman girls, Risa Yamanaka and Tatsuko Nonaka, on their birthdays, because they requested it. I took perhaps my tenth photograph with the breathtaking freshman Amazoness Wakako Endo, alone in the room after class, her phenomenally protuberant left breast grazing my forearm, because she insisted on doing it. And as for E-mail innuendo, Yuriko is going at least as far in her messages to me as I have ever gone with her or anybody else. I could give further examples in this vein.

October 1997

<u>October 1997</u>: A meeting attended by <u>Newsweek</u>'s Michael Isikoff, Lucianne and Jonah Goldberg, and Ms. Tripp was held at Mr. Goldberg's apartment in Washington. A tape of the Tripp/Lewinsky conversations was played.

—◻—

I attended [the NU Cultural Festival] *two days this year and, as always, had all the junk food my colon could bear. As usual, I saw some good jazz performances—Emi Denda on her damn trombone.... Next door, the DJ club had a huge classroom and absolutely nothing to do in it, so they played my albums really loud on powerful speakers.*

November 1997

November 1997: Finding herself alone in the study
with the President, Ms. Lewinsky gave him a
paperweight in the shape of the White House. She
then mentioned an email she had seen purporting
that chewing Altoid mints prior to performing
fellatio could enhance the pleasure of the act.
(She was chewing Altoids at this time.) The
President kissed her but said there was no time
for fellatio, and then hurried to a State Dinner
for Mexican President Zedillo.

In a perfect world, President Clinton, Monica Lewinsky, Emi Denda and I would star in a sitcom called *No Time for Fellatio*.

—◻—

On Friday, I cut loose at an Amataro party with one of my sophomore classes, organized by Shigeru Kato. It was "the boring group"... I got to stand really, really close to Mayumi Nishida while taking a Print Club picture. I attempted to set the suddenly voluble and irritating Kenta Sumida on fire. I roused normally somnambulant Minoru Tachibana by indicating to him that the salaryman who had been using the urinal next to his had been masturbating. I got into a furious, unprovoked fistfight with metalhead dweeb Yuta Ichihara... I was, in short, on top of my game in spite of sleep deprivation, and then slept until 3 the next afternoon.

Classes got to be more and more fun as the year entered its final phase.

91

Wakako humors me by giving me more pictures of herself for my collection. I kissed a couple more girls, but I worried that they were simply falling into line, afraid of "standing out" by taking the gum [on their birthdays] *instead of the kiss. But I liked kissing them nonetheless.*

November 1997

December 1997: An officer mentioned to Ms. Lewinsky that Eleanor Mondale was in the White House. Ms. Lewinsky supposed that the President was with Ms. Mondale, not his lawyers, and she became "livid." She left the White House, placed an angry phone call to Ms. Currie from a pay phone, and then returned to her apartment.

[The freshman] *party on the 5th...was a small affair, but included four women and one guy whom I have kissed. I sprang for 10,000 yen of the bill, worth every cent of it for the thrill of sitting next to the fabulous Wakako Endo and guessing her weight.*

December 1997

December 17, 1997: Lawyers for Paula Jones, then suing the President on sexual harassment charges, subpoenaed Ms. Lewinsky.

December 28, 1997: On her final visit to the White House, Ms. Lewinsky was signed in by Ms. Currie. When Ms. Lewinsky met privately with the President, he allegedly coached her on how to be evasive in her answers in the Jones lawsuit.

Stay tuned for another episode of *No Time for Fellatio.*

...But Clinton Was
Still Going Strong

...But DiMaggio was still going strong...on his own record, now.
Would he hit safely in every game forever? It seemed that way.
And why not? He was only 26 and playing baseball in the sunshine.
He heard little boys cheer, not cry.

—Philip Marlowe, 1975 movie adaptation of *Farewell, My Lovely*

HI! Muggins!

How are you ? Akemashite Omedetou gozaimas. [Happy New Year.] *I am surviving in fukin' Worthless College.** *I saw your home page at the November. My photo was not so good but it was O.K...*

Any way how is everything going? I just got backed from christmas vacation. I went to Mexico city and El Paso and New Orleans... Mexico city was really crowded and polluted. some people was really nice but some people was really bad. I was stolen my CD case (there were 12 CDs in there) FUCK!!! However I enjoyed ruins.

At the New Orleans I met Rei Uchiumi. She seemed to have fun in San Diego. We had a really good time in there. I Looooove New Orleans!!!! I went to Jazz club every night and ate cajuan food every day. Since I was always surrounded by white people , it was good refreshment for me to go to New

---

* A play on the name of the small Midwestern liberal arts institution to which she had been sentenced for a year.

Orleans and surrounded by black people.

Last semster was pretty hard for me. I was almost dying every day. I had one English class and two poli-Scie classs and Jazz dance. I had to write many papers and to read many books. Also I lived in dormitory It was really damn and my room mate was sooo boring for me. This semster I moved to cottage. I hope it will work well. study was really tough for me but my grade was not so bad as I expected (my GPA was 3.2)

Worthless College is worthless than I expected. [The town] *is damn too. There are only white and christian and republican people are living here. I always feel that I am eilian or somethig like that. Every one is crazy about Jejus. Since I am not so religious person, I always feel guilty. I am getting to do not like Hakujin* [white people] *more. However there are nice student, I made friend with them but most of them,,,are not interested in other than Worthless. They are concept of world is really narrow for me....*

I am O.K. because I am Nangaku great woman. Any way I miss every thing in Japan. (friends , boy friend, family, food, of course Muggins!!) I want to write more but I should stop here.

Keep in touch. I am looking forward to your response.

LOVE
Honami

January 12, 1998: Whitewater Independent Counsel Ken Starr was informed of the tapes made by Ms. Tripp. Allegedly, Ms. Lewinsky could be heard on the tapes offering details of her affair with the President and implying that the President and his friend Vernon Jordan advised her to lie about the affair under oath.

January 13, 1998: Ms. Tripp and Ms. Lewinsky met at a hotel bar in Pentagon City, Virginia. Ms. Tripp, wired by FBI agents, recorded the encounter.

—□—

I've had my share of fun this month—pelting groovy freshman babes with snowballs and so on. I'm writing recommendation letters right and left. Asada babes gave me a slick faux-silk bathrobe with a huge shiny tiger on it. Thanks to genius geek Numabe's advice, I've got the photos on my home page loading faster and prettier than ever.

In short, I still worry about the year. But now more than ever I have faith in the credo, "There's no such thing as a bad year at Nangaku."

January 1998

Anyway, I was having a better year at that point than the President was.

January 26, 1998: "Now, I have to go back to work on my State of the Union speech. And I worked on it until pretty late last night. But I want to say one thing to the American people. I want you to listen to me. I'm going to say this again: I did not have sexual relations with that woman, Miss Lewinsky. I never told anybody to lie, not a single time; never. These allegations are false. And I need to go back to work for the American people. Thank you."

—□—

Numerous people who hinted at visiting me have failed to do so. Yuriko did come over on the 11th along with Kazue Inoue. They listened to my new songs with no sign of visible emotion…. Yuriko has a boyfriend.

After they left, I drank a bottle of wine alone. And had another bottle of wine on Friday. And another last night. This is looking bad.

March 1998

Yes, but again, I could always take solace in one thing: Life was looking even worse for the President of the United States of America.

February 6, 1998: The President rejected the notion that he resign because of the accusations against him. At a news conference, he said he would never "walk away from the people of this country and the trust they've placed in me."

March 10, 1998: A grand jury heard four hours of testimony from former White House volunteer Kathleen Willey, who alleged that the President had subjected her to unwanted physical contact.

—◻—

Momoko Sakuta is back from New Zealand. I hugged her and felt her large breasts. Eri Kuramochi is back from there, too. I hugged her.

April 1998

Oh, ha-ha, I probably thought while writing that. *I really slammed ol' Eri Kuramochi and her relative lack of boobage. That'll teach a girl to fob off a bony-chested hug on me. Yep, Eri Kuramochi—destined by flat-chestedness to the dustbin of NU history.*

And yet, and yet...years later, it is the cantilevered Momoko who jiggles blurrily in my memory, while I get perfect reception on Eri Kuramochi, for three reasons.

1. Eri Kuramochi had magnificent buttocks.

She was in the cycling club and used to spend vacations with her mates on long treks through rural Japan. One day, while cycling home from school, I found myself several meters behind her as she pumped fluidly away, oblivious to my presence, her asscheeks rising and falling by turns like the bulbous heads of Tweedle-dum and Tweedle-dee; and it was, as noted above, magnificent. I labored to keep up with her so as to maintain that view as long as possible, but she effortlessly pulled away from me at the next hill. In my defense, her bike had gears.

2. No one overcame more setbacks to studying abroad.

That was her dream from the get-go—specifically to go to a University of California campus. She took my TOEFL intensive course as soon as she was eligible, then took it again. And then again. Her scores were miserable and barely ticked upward.

I would hand back a practice test to her with as much enthusiasm as if I were serving her an eviction notice. I would watch her brow crinkle, see her fight back tears, and then somehow pull through it. I would write encouraging fortune-cookie blurbs on those score sheets—*A breakthrough is just around the corner! Not all improvement is visible in scores! You'll get 'em next time!*—that, just between you and me, I rarely felt.

Year by year, she cheerfully saw off clusters of classmates who qualified for the UC exchange. Like an adorable, bulb-butted George Bailey, Eri always stayed behind. She volunteered for the buddy program to associate with the foreign students who came to NU. She took all my electives. She quit cycling to focus more on English. When her score nudged just high enough to meet the application requirement, she applied—and was rejected. So she applied again. And again.

She never did conquer the competitive UC selection but made it to New Zealand for a year, though she had to postpone graduation.

3. And then, there's this.

At her belated graduation in March of the following year, a red-kimono-clad Eri pulled me aside for a photo op. As we posed, these words passed between us.

"What are you going to do now, Eri?"

"I'm going on to nursing school. I'm gonna be a nurse!"

"Really? Oh, that's great."

She leaned close just before we were snapped and whispered, "So I can take care of you when you get old."

Well… That just wasn't fair, was it?

—¤—

In April 1998, we all began a school year for the first time armed with the knowledge that even the President of the United States could be undone by his own hormones.

They seem so young and naive, even by freshman standards. Where are the preternaturally knowing girls like Ren Akiba or Shoko Namiki? (Well, there is a girl named Yuika Sekine who looks like she's been taken for a ride by more than one test-driver. But apart from her, the whole class could very well consist of virgins.) Their E-mail messages are pleasant and sweet. They lend me their favorite CDs and bake little sweets for me. They're just too, too good for the lascivious likes of me, and yet I love them anyway.

May 1998

Like the President, you see, I was sometimes seized by these weird, unbidden urges to become a better man. And then the moment would pass.

99

Well, at the nitty-gritty, day-to-day level, life still unfolds in a highly agreeable way... Recently I have become an E-mail Ann Landers, giving advice to the lovelorn, both male and female. Ha!—little do they imagine that they correspond with a tit-obsessed middle-aged pervert. Riko Kamiya, noted married-man-fucker and study-abroad hopeful, is my most faithful correspondent of late.

June 1998

—◻—

August 17, 1998: After becoming the first sitting president to testify before a grand jury, President Bill Clinton went on national TV to admit he had a "not appropriate" relationship with Monica Lewinsky.

Meanwhile, I was in full-on pompous composer/arranger mode once again.

Satsuki came back on the 23rd with Mieko and we did a pretty fair [duet]. *I might ask her to come over and do it again. She's nothing if not reliable. She's my great new love and, I'm both surprised and proud to say, there isn't a shred of sexual attraction among the many ingredients of my affection for her. Have I matured? Or just learned from the example of Bill Clinton? Satsuki is cute and pretty, but I really do just love her for the wonderful friend that she has become. After recording, we had lunch at MosBurger.*

September 1998

Satsuki and Mieko reinforced my long-standing theory that NU sophomore chicks were God's most perfect creations. Scrawny, wholesome girls, they had shed the shyness of their freshman days but had not yet outgrown me.

The recording session described above was the first since I had moved to my new, larger apartment, nestled in the same lush, bamboo-forested valley below the campus where many of the students found off-campus housing—the area I came to call Nangaku Land.*

—◻—

September 21, 1998: More than four hours of President Clinton's videotaped grand jury testimony was released by the House Judiciary Committee and subsequently broadcast on many television networks. Also released were over 3000 pages of testimony and evidence, including a photo of the semen-stained dress.

That fall, I used a news video and essay to introduce sexual harassment from an American perspective in one of my read-and-discuss classes. On the follow-up writing exercise, I offered an optional question that allowed students to recount any episode of sexual harassment that they themselves might have experienced or witnessed. Here is the most cherished response, reconstructed from memory, by a cheerful, bug-eyed IR freshman.

Last year, when I was a third-year student in high school, my homeroom teacher told my friend and me that we had to come back to his room in the evening, after our club activity. When we came back, there was no one else around, and our teacher had taken off his shirt. He got down on his hands and knees and said, "Why don't you ride on my back? Come on!" My friend and I were very surprised. We said, "Sorry, but we have to study," and ran away.

---

* In other news, there really is a Japanese fast-food chain whose name is pronounced "moss burger." It is not bad.

Yes. They apologized and made a polite excuse. Of course they did.

— ◻ —

October 8, 1998: The House of Representatives voted 258-176 in favor of authorizing an inquiry into the possible impeachment of President Clinton. The inquiry was supported by 31 Democrats.

Two weeks later, on my birthday:

Wakako Endo kissed me on request (also, on the head). Mieko and Satsuki bought me lunch, immediately after which Sumina Nishibara and Tatsuko Nonaka shaved my head. This was interrupted briefly by the appearance of the one freshman who was on the ball, Michiko Sunagawa. In short, I was in Nangaku Woman heaven. Moreover, until Takuro Fujita showed up 20 minutes late, I was the only stud present in the third period class.

October 1998

In the commemorative photo, Wakako Endo (aka the Amazoness) is indeed kissing me on the head as I bend down to give her easier access. One also notes that both of her hands are balled into fists, as if she has reserved until the last instant her right to choose between kissing me and pummeling me into unconsciousness. As the daughter of a prominent retired professional athlete, she was eminently capable of the latter. Looking back, I wish we could have done both.

Azusa Hoshino came over on Saturday to get oriented for the recording of "Nangaku Land." She brought old recording comrades... It was a fun night of giddy inanity, and the girls, having just had their yearbook pictures taken that afternoon, looked more gorgeous than ever. But we didn't get much done besides devour a lot of pizza.

October 1998

When the sliding *shoji* doors dividing the living room and bedroom of my new and larger apartment were opened, one could skip in a circle formed by those rooms plus the kitchen. This is exactly what the elfin soprano Azusa and her friends—three equally Barbie-like English majors of the type Toko had once accused of having no nipples—were doing when the pizza arrived.

"This place is so big, we could all just *live* here with you!" Azusa cooed right on cue, dumbfounding the pizza dude.

> October 28, 1998: Republicans released TV ads about the President's affair with Monica Lewinsky as the 1998 Congressional races wound down.

Finally, I had all the ingredients I needed. Satsuki and Mieko came over on the 22nd and helped me assemble over 80 albums. I'd cut off a finger for either of those girls and do it smilingly.

October 1998

> November 1998: Independent Counsel Ken Starr stated that President Clinton consistently "chose deception" while summarizing his case against the President before the House Judiciary Committee.

—◻—

When I'm at Nangaku on a typical bright, shiny, hectic day, surrounded by the beauty of the campus and that of so many of its inhabitants, nothing else seems to matter. I'm in heaven, and I'm Muggins! But at other times, my life doesn't seem nearly so cool. And the future hovers ahead like a cold black hole in space. These days, every time I make a slightly gratuitous purchase—real champagne for the [album release] *party last week as opposed to cheaper "sparkling wine," for example—I see in my mind a time when I struggle to muster the coins to pay the electric bill.*

December 1998

December 19, 1998: The House of Representatives approved two articles of impeachment after two days of debate. The articles accused the President of lying under oath and obstructing justice.

They sent me (and every other teacher, I presume) a lengthy questionnaire on the sexual harassment issue less than a week after I got the word on Russ. It provided lively fodder for my Great Women of Nangaku interview with Mai Onuma. It was a good time.

December 1998

—□—

A dominant theme in both global and local news that fall of 1998 was sexual harassment.

There was the President, of course. While it was, somewhat ironically, an entirely consensual affair that almost destroyed him, the groundwork for that scandal had been laid by rumors over the years of his making a nuisance of himself to various women in various despicable ways. At NU, meanwhile, we had Russ, a full professor in the English Department.

"Full" doesn't quite cover it; he was, like Falstaff, a gross, fat, and highly excitable man of advancing years, but without the thought-provoking soliloquies or roguish relatability. Not an English Department person myself, I was one of the last to get the proverbial memo that Russ was being slowly and excruciatingly crowbarred out of his position after a senior accused him of offering her one of those *quid pro quo*s we were hearing so much about in those days.

First they came for the fat and pompous English Department full professors, and I was not a fat and pompous English Department full professor, so I did not speak out. And then they came for and-so-forth-and-so-on, and I did not etc., etc., but enough pretentious literary references.

Even a creature of my ilk could see that some guidelines needed to be set, as there was abundant anecdotal evidence to suggest that many of my faculty brethren were coping with the estrogen-heavy NU atmosphere even less professionally than I was.

—◻—

Way back in 1990, my very first year at NU, I met Dan, a Japanese "returnee" who had spent his entire K-12 education in suburban Chicago-area schools. "Hey man, I'm just tryin' to wrap my head around this freakin' place," he said to me on our mutual first day of class when I asked why he seemed so inattentive. I took to the lad at once.

Some years later, he told me of another class he had attended on that very same traumatizing first day of school in his native land:

So, it was one of those big lecture halls in Building 6. I got there early so I just sat near the front. I didn't know anything, like how Japanese students always sit as far back as they can. So the room filled up but everybody was at least three rows behind me. And then I noticed that all the girls were sittin' on one side of the room and all the guys on the other side. What's up with that shit?

Anyway, I just sat there waiting for, like, twenty minutes, and finally the guy comes in, little old bald guy in a ratty suit, probably forty-something.

And he just starts talkin' about, you know, normal stuff: the syllabus, the textbook, how we'll be graded, that kinda shit. I'm not payin' much attention after a while, and then suddenly I realize that he's been sayin' shit like, "You don't have to be shy about sex. Sex is the most natural thing in the world! Everybody has sex, you know. You look at TV, you see politicians, judges in a courtroom, all these serious people, but they ALL have sex" and blah blah blah. "We all have to be naked sometimes," that sort of crap.

I turn around, and all the girls are, like, cringing back in their seats, just tryin' to get a little farther away from this guy, but he just keeps goin' on like that even after the bell.

I asked what kind of class it had been—biology, I supposed.

"Fuck if I remember. Constitutional law or some shit like that."

—◻—

Perhaps the reader begins to grasp how, in such an environment, someone like me could regard himself as a bona fide moderate, behaving-in-a-classroom-full-of-young-Japanese-ladies-wise.

Thus, it was only mildly alarming to receive a questionnaire by mail from the newly formed NU Committee on Sexual Harassment and Human Rights. No, let me back up: It was *extremely* alarming to receive a thick envelope by mail from the NU Committee on Sexual Harassment and Human Rights.

The envelope's exterior gave no indication that it was a mass mailing to all faculty, leading me to suspect something more personal, like a twelve-pack of affidavits signed by students dating back to 1990, possibly including Dan.

It really threw me off my preparations for my dinner date that evening with the brilliant Mai Onuma, a petite and comely junior just back from her year abroad at UC Berkeley, who had agreed to suffer through a Great Women of Nangaku interview.

But then I decided to make lemonade from this lemon—i.e., to use the questionnaire as interview fodder.

—◻—

By the time we got around to the sexual harassment questionnaire, I had told Mai that she was a very beautiful woman and extracted her weight (a hundred and one pounds on a five-feet-one-inch frame) and her evaluation of her own sex drive ("About average, I guess"). Meanwhile, she had firmly but gently corrected me as to which fork I was supposed to use, further proving, if proof be needed, her Greatness.

The questionnaire posited various scenarios and asked us to judge each one as:

(a) Serious sexual harassment
(b) Mild sexual harassment
(c) Not sexual harassment

I asked Mai to read the questionnaire items and translate as needed. Here are excerpts from the interview:

Mai: "Item 1: Without necessity, someone requests sex from another person."

Me: So, there are cases where this sort of request is necessary?

Mai: Hmm, it's a little strange...

Me: So for example, if I said, "Excuse me, young lady. I'm suffering from a rare disease. I really hate to ask you this but—"

Mai: I'm not convinced of your necessity...

Me: The answer for this one has to be (a).

Mai: Agreed. "Item 2: A person stares in a sexually meaningful way at another person's chest, buttocks, legs, etc."

Me: So, not touching? Just looking?

Mai: Yes, but looking for a long time, so…

Me: I'm going with (c) here. It's rude but not harassment. What say you?

Mai: I can't quite give this an (a), but certainly a (b).

Me: Oh…really? A (b)… Well, you know, it's not really on purpose—

Mai: [Uncomfortable laughter]

Me: Sometimes it really can't be helped, what with the things they wear nowadays.

Mai: To be sure, the exposure level is getting higher.

Me: In summer, especially, when they sit right in the front row—

Mai: Let's move on. "Saying things like 'Women always quit their jobs anyway, so they don't have to look for work.'"

Me: You mean, like, a professor saying that in class?

Mai: Right.

Me: Frankly, I'd have to respect any man who said that to an International Relations class. I mean…

Mai: [Sincere laughter]

Me: …there'd be girls waiting for him in the parking lot that night.

Mai: Yeah, there are plenty of powerful women around here.

Me: So, what do you think? Sexual harassment?

Mai: Hmm... Between an (a) and a (b). I'll go with (b).

Me: Really?

Mai: Yeah. The guy has a biased viewpoint.

Me: I make a distinction between sexism and sexual harassment. This guy is a sexist, but... I'm going with (c).

Mai: "Persistently asking someone to have dinner together or go on a date"... [Gasps]

Me: [Holding breath.]

Mai: You weren't persistent, so I didn't mind.

Me: Because you said okay. To be honest, I intended to persist if you at first said "No thanks."

Mai: [Nervous laughter]

Me: At the same time, I admit that it's despicable. This one's between an (a) and a (b).

Mai: Yeah, I agree.*

Me: But you know, when we were making my latest album together,

---

* In retrospect, I'm fairly certain that Mai was downgrading most of her answers out of consideration for the feelings of her hopelessly out-of-touch dinner-buying companion.

I persistently demanded that Yuriko come over to my apartment.

Mai: Have you received any email from Yuri-chan?[*]

Me: Just a little. She seems to be very busy. I sent her the finished album, and she wrote back to say "Thank you for the album. I'm busy. Goodbye." That's all.

Mai: I can appreciate how busy she is.

Me: She helped tremendously on that album. When it was nearly finished, we had an appointment at my apartment, but she got sick. So I just kept sending her faxes: "Come here now and record our song with me!" and she would fax back "I can't, I have a fever." But I said, "I don't care! Come here now!" I suppose that might be sexual harassment.

Mai: [Fidgeting]

Me: So, what's next?

Mai: Next is, "Talking about a female student's body, clothing, or sexual relationships in the presence of others."

Me: Ahh…

Mai: Well, this is certainly an (a).

Me: I'm ashamed to tell you, but I actually did this recently.

Mai: You did?

Me: Yeah. It was at a year-end party for the people who helped with my album. There were three girls and three or four guys there. I was pretty drunk and…

---

[*] Yuriko was by then safely in San Diego for her year abroad.

—¤—

Basuto bijin was the term I had used at the party. I had been seeing it in eye-catching ads for seedy magazines on trains, and just had to try out this new addition to my Japanese vocabulary. It translates roughly as "busty beauty," and, it turns out, has precisely the creepy-uncle-izing effect on the user that you would expect it to.

A boy named Shigeru was lamenting his single status. I suggested he make a move on a classmate named Nami, not in attendance that evening but well known to all who were. "I like that Nami," I enthused, "she's a real *basuto bijin!*"

Immediately, every female in attendance fell silent and dropped her chin so as to examine her own chest, then folded her arms over it.

My "bust bijin" comment will not soon be forgotten by the female attendees. But I suspect Satsuki and Mieko will forgive me, after all we've been through.

December 1998

—¤—

January 7, 1999: The Senate began the trial of President Bill Clinton by swearing in Chief Justice William Rehnquist to preside.

January 18 was the last regular class day of the year. I was back in fine fettle for it, but still went down twice in arm-wrestling. Well, I sort of took a dive for Yukino Tsuino, who really needed that bonus point to put her over the top. But Moeka Yamagishi flat out whipped my ass.

111

The second class (Michiko Sunagawa et al) put on a nice little ceremony for me as soon as Akimi Torii's dubious Muggins impersonation was over. It featured formal thank-you speeches by Kunihiko and Mamoru and the presenting of a nice sweater vest.

January 1999

Editor's note: The above journal entry marks the last day that I would have Michiko in my class. Within a week, she and I would, without making any pretense of "necessity," segue into a thoroughly gelatinous and clandestine fifteen-month love affair— the only such relationship I would ever experience with an NU woman.

Those fifteen months were rife with titillating stories full of exceedingly intimate details, but I will not share any of them with the general public.*

But as we move forward, please bear in mind that it was here, in early 1999, just as the President was getting his comeuppance for his own excesses with a much younger woman, and just as NU was belatedly sorting through its surplus of oversexed male teachers and chucking out the rotten ones, that I embarked on this affair.

And now I need to go back to work for the Japanese people. Thank you.

February 12, 1999: The impeachment trial of
President Clinton ended in acquittal. The
President was found not guilty of perjury by a
vote of 55-45. The Senators were evenly divided on
the charge of obstruction of justice.

—◻—

On Friday night, Sumina and Tatsuko came over with Saori Fukushi At

* Having already blabbed them all in an earlier memoir.

their own expense they (mainly Sumina) whipped up a fabulous full-course Italian dinner which we downed with two bottles of wine and plenty of gossip about errant UC boys.* It was fun, and in a normal month of May would have been by far the most excitement I could ever hope to have with Nangaku girls. But the bar that defines "excitement" has been changed, and I wonder if I'll ever get it back down where it belongs.

May 1999

July 29, 1999: The President was ordered to pay $90,686 by U.S. District Court Judge Susan Webber for giving false testimony in the civil sexual harassment lawsuit against him by Paula Jones.

I finally managed to modernize my home page with some accouterments like a counter and a survey in which people can vote. The current topic is "how my Nangaku career will ultimately end." In sparse voting so far, "happy retirement at a ripe old age in Hawaii" is in a dead heat with "forced to resign in a sex scandal."

September 1999

That was gallows humor given the fact that word of The Relationship was already leaking around campus. Over summer vacation, the girlfriend and I had been IDed by the estimable Wakako Endo in the midst of some particularly childish PDA at a popular dating spot in central Yokohama. After school began again, I sensed a chilliness in some old friends.

I saw Satsuki Mori and Mieko Iwasawa eating lunch outdoors and sat down with them. Satsuki turned to me and coldly asked how I could say "I

---

* Visiting University of California students.

love you" to so many girls. The name Wakako Endo was later invoked, leaving little doubt in my mind what Satsuki was talking about. The proverbial cat was out of the proverbial bag...

It's the potential for damage to my friendship with Satsuki, as well as Wakako Endo and God knows how many others by now, that nags at me. A few days later I called Satsuki at home and had this conversation:

Me: I have something I want to talk to you about. Are you busy now?

Satsuki: Actually, I am.

October 1999

I would have fretted for my job as well, but for the "1.5-year Rule." Through rigorous scientific observation, I had determined that, whenever a juicy news item permeated the International Relations student body, it took exactly eighteen months for that information to leech its way up the ivy to where the regular faculty wafted. It was as constant and reliable as the mating cycle of the Pacific walrus. So I had some wiggle room there, walrus-wise.

—◻—

August 18, 1999: The federal court panel that appointed Independent Counsel Ken Starr voted 2-1 to keep his office going.

The last morning of freshman classes was particularly moving this year. The first period class—the one I had grown rather weary of—chipped in and bought me a very expensive sweater. They also provided individual cards and notes, which I have not read yet. A makeshift troupe of five boys grabbed a bonus point in the Muggins Mimicry Challenge by donning plastic bald heads and stringy white beards, and going through a series of synchronized gestures and catch-phrases and maniacal laughter. And they all came over and kissed me, to boot.

The second period group gave me a grab-bag of weird stuff a mushroom-growing piece of wood, an apron, a ski mask, a new whistle... I put them all on at once and became a wood-brandishing terrorist cleaning lady.

January 2000

—◻—

Tonight, once again following a Princess visit, I set out for a drinking party near Yokohama Station with the* [freshman] *class. Narumi Suzuki accused me of sexual harassment for no reason, then kissed me twice. Sanae Kayama told me more than I expected to hear about her date with Junya "Girl Magnet" Nozawa, and then touched my cock. (Both actions were accidental.) I was tired, but I had fun.*

January 2000

The new and much publicized sexual harassment policy, fortified by the public examples made of some violators, soon achieved its intended effect of making NU girls feel secure. Really, really secure. Overnight, it seemed to me, the NU campus had been transformed into one large gentlemen's club VIP room, where scantily-clad vixens operated under the rubric "I can touch you, but you can't touch me."

—◻—

I am not sure if this constitutes an act of sexual harassment against NU women. If it does, then the entire university was complicit in it. If not, it still merits preserving here as one of the greatest unsolved mysteries I have witnessed.

In February, while teaching one of my intensive courses, I happened to walk along a covered passageway that ran just outside

---

* Nickname of girlfriend. Yes, I know: "Never date a girl whose father calls her Princess." Where were you when I needed you, eh?

115

the building housing most of our large lecture halls. There, against the wall facing the doors to one such hall, someone had propped up a blackboard that had apparently been removed from said hall.

The reason for the removal was easily surmised: someone had permanently defaced the twelve-foot green slab by painting a series of eight disembodied, upward-pointing white boners across it. Reading left to right, the first boner measured about twelve inches; the second perhaps sixteen inches; and so it went in a carefully calibrated arithmetic progression.

The longer boners were no greater in girth than the shorter ones, giving the tableau a calliope vibe. But the analogy falls apart when one recalls that a calliope can only emit sound from a limited number of its pipes at any moment, whereas here, every single one of these anonymous needledicks was spewing its contents simultaneously into the air, like an upside-down sprinkler system dousing a warehouse fire.

The decision to plant the blackboard there, out in the open, was forgivable, I felt. Surely the disposal of something so large was no easy matter and required a few days' planning; and in the meantime, few students would be subjected to the sight owing to the long winter break.

But one month later, when my second intensive course began, there it remained. And a few weeks after that came orientation, followed by the start of the new academic year.

Now hundreds of students, mostly female, were daily faced with the prospect of a head-on collision with what I had begun calling Cock Stonehenge (since the artist had not deigned to title it) as they emerged from that lecture hall. Add to that the few hundred more who used the covered walkway to get to their next class—a number that tripled on rainy days—and our unknown artist was getting more free exposure than a minivan full of reality TV stars.

There it sat, and sat, and spurted, and spurted, uncommented upon and unapproached. Occasionally male passersby would snarkily point it out to each other, but no one lingered at the scene:

no one wanted to risk the collective wrath of NU womanhood by seeming to endorse it.

Surely the cocks had by this time drawn the attention of regular faculty and staff as well, and I yearned to ask someone about it. But owing to my menial status, the only person I could have approached was the kindly, motherly secretary who didn't get out of the IR office much. I imagined our conversation thusly:

Me: Say, aren't they ever going to do anything about that blackboard out there?

Secretary: What blackboard?

And right there she would have me checkmated, my remaining moves limited to:

(a) Saying to this gentle soul, who sometimes brought rice-balls for me when she thought I was losing too much weight, "The one with all the spurting cocks—check it out!" or

(b) Sheepishly walking away.

In the end, I decided not to risk it.

Over the summer, at least two Open Campus events were held for high school students and their parents, and I saw no efforts made to so much as temporarily cover Cock Stonehenge. And there it stayed through Christmas season, seeming to mock the nearby bust of our Puritan founder.

The following winter, around the anniversary of its debut, I again found myself peering into the piece while no one else was around. It was tucked under a low overhang, which made it difficult but not impossible to approach. By this time, I had begun to marvel that the administration had not roped it off or glassed it in, so intent on maintaining it they seemed to be.

Screwing my courage to the sticking point, I resolved to step in and touch it. But this led to a new dilemma: when a work of art consists entirely of spurting cocks, there are really only two options for the would-be toucher to touch: (a) a cock, or (b) cock-spurt. Either course required an unshakable comfort with one's own sexual identity, which at forty-five I did not yet possess.

I opted for spurt, and for that of the smallest cock, thinking this the course least likely to enrage whatever Phallic Gods might be protecting this shrine. The spurt smeared.

It was chalk. Or perhaps it had been cheap paint, but long exposure to elements had powderized it. In my eagerness to test this theory, I absent-mindedly licked the spurt from my fingers and then went for a random cock, which smeared just as easily. The whole monument could easily be eradicated with half a roll of Bounty.

A few weeks later the blackboard vanished, with no more explanation than when it had appeared.

"Group psych experiment" is the best guess I can give you.

—□—

March 13, 2000: After a six-year investigation of President Clinton and first lady Hillary Rodham Clinton, Whitewater Independent Counsel Robert Ray started filing final reports.

The turn of the millennial clock signaled the winding down of the Clinton scandals. Indeed, there was less than a year to go in the Clinton presidency, a notion that could only come as a relief even to those of us who still admired the President, if only for his stamina. It likewise marked my shift, starting April 1, to full-time employment, for IR had made me a contract offer that I could not refuse.

It also signaled the end of my idyllic but doomed relationship with Michiko, which would collapse faster than an Italian coalition government during the Golden Week holidays in early May, five weeks into the new school year. My own collapse followed apace.

I will not bore the reader with all the deranged, whiny, suicidal and inexcusable behavior that I indulged myself in off and on for the next two years.[*] Let's just say that I found insanity highly overrated, and move on.

— ◻ —

On the 21st, after coming home from my colon-cancer check, I got a phone call from [freshman] Kazuyo Mashiko inviting me to a drinking party with her class. I went there, drank too much (on top of the anesthesia still coursing through me), took off a lot of my clothes, made obscene phone calls to girls' boyfriends, and engaged in what I actually took to be serious negotiations for taking Mai Ichihara with me to Okinawa for diving lessons.

July 2000

— ◻ —

August 17, 2000: A new grand jury investigating the scandal involving President Clinton and White House intern Monica Lewinsky was impaneled in July by Independent Counsel Robert Ray, according to CNN.

In the final years of his term, following the first reports of his affair with an intern, President Clinton formalized peace in Northern Ireland, bombed the Serbs out of Kosovo, launched

---

[*] Having already done so in that earlier memoir.

initiatives to tighten regulation of nursing homes and reduce elementary school class sizes, funded the hiring of 100,000 new police officers, expanded the Violence Against Women Act, and achieved three consecutive budget surpluses, each nearly double the size of the one before.

Thus, as I rode the Floo Network through two years of ineffective counseling and drugs (prescribed and other), my whispered mantra, sponged from a dimly remembered movie, became:

But Clinton is still going strong.

—◻—

There were manic moments as well, to be sure: I gave a live performance at a school festival that was generally well-received[*]; and continued to crawl out of bed every day to teach my assigned classes, after a fashion.

The conversational point in class one October day was "asking for and giving advice." Language to be activated included, "I'm having a few problems" and "I wonder if you could give me some advice?" and "You should do such and such," or "If I were you, I'd do this-and-that."

I put the students in groups of four, had them write summaries of three or four of their problems on cards, and then set those cards in the middle of the group, to be turned over and discussed one by one.

As I circulated, I noticed that one group appeared stymied. "What's the matter here?" I asked.

Freshman Girl: We don't know what to tell Akio.

Me: Akio, what is your problem?

---

[*] Turns out not caring much whether you live or die lends itself to successful live performances. Who knew?

Akio: I can't find a girlfriend. I wonder if you could give me some advice?

Me: Sure. Well, if your target is NU girls, I think the key point is to lay back a little.

Akio: Oh?

Me: Yes. Your typical NU girl doesn't like a guy who comes on strong.

Akio: Uh-huh.

Me: At least, that's been my experience.

Akio: Ahh…

Me: I'm not saying be mean to them or anything like that. You smile at them, you say good morning…

Akio: Okay.

Me: …But never, ever give them any reason to believe that you *need* them.

Akio: Ah.

Me: Because once they know that you *need* them, you're doomed. Doomed, I tell you.

Akio: Oh.

Me: Your attitude should always be, like, "I don't need you. I like you, I hope you like me. But I absolutely don't *need* you."

Akio: Really?

Me: Yes. You keep up that attitude, and you'll have dozens of 'em flocking to you.

At this point I turned off my laser-like focus on Akio and noticed for the first time that the three female members of the group had been gaping slack-jawed at me with an emotion of unknown provenance. I excused myself and moved on to supervise another group. Over my shoulder, I heard Akio say:
"I don't *need* you."

— □ —

Kazuyo Mashiko barely speaks to me anymore. I have no idea what she's pissed about, but I'm sure she could build a pretty compelling sexual harassment case against me if she wanted to.

November 2000

I suppose I was thinking of the time I had regained consciousness in her apartment at two-thirty in the morning, but in my defense it was she and her friends who dragged me there, for lack of alternatives. Never a night deposit slot for drunken teachers nearby when you need one.

Dear Muggins,

Hi! How are you? I'm fine.
I recieved your e-mail. And I read what you worry about.

>I sometimes worry that you are disappointed in me recently.
>Maybe you think my strange behavior while drinking is too much.
> Well, I can't apologize for the kind of person that I am.
> As you know, I'm just a middle-aged child.

> *However, if I did or said anything to you, personally, which made you uncomfortable, I do apologize for it.*

I don't know what is that. You worry about your drinking behavior? you don't need to care about it. It is natural that the person drink a lot. and become a drunken man. and me too.

By the way, I went to the NU Cultural Festival for 3 days.
I sold Cha-han as a circle. I tried to make a Cha-han only one time.
It is taste good. It is easy for every one to make a Cha-han.
Have you ever made it?
Cha-han raised good fame. so we could sell all of them! after that, we went to drink. it was almost free!
now I have to do your home work(academic writing) it is hard!

Kazuyo

—¤—

December 8, 2000: Manual recounts were ordered in some counties by the Florida Supreme Court in response to Gore's appeal. Bush then appealed to the U.S. Supreme Court to stop the recounts.

December 9, 2000: The U.S. Supreme Court voted 5-4 to halt the hand recounts.

That wild and woolly freshman class invited me to yet another get-together, this one a house party at Shintaro Kitaura's place. I engaged in simulated anal intercourse with Takafumi.

December 2000

With all due respect to Takafumi's anus, I remember this one mainly as "that party where Kazuyo Mashiko excused herself, stepped outside, vomited repeatedly on her hands and knees, then returned to the party and calmly resumed drinking."

That girl was poised. If we ever need to confront visiting aliens, we need her right out front.

—□—

Shortly after the new year, I was summoned to another party, this one arranged by some non-IR seniors whose study-abroads of the previous year I had facilitated.

It was held at a bar and populated mainly by geeks, thus greatly mitigating any possibility of anal sex real or faux, but I had a good time anyway—or at least, as good a time as I was capable of having in my still depressive and oft-sedated state.

There were just two lads and I at first, and the early highlight was Michitaka's reminiscence of being interrupted by his American roommate in the throes of amusing himself to a rented porno. The story's climax brought forth much geeky guffawing, but the mood altered quickly—becoming warmer and less spastic—when we were joined by Junko, a squat, bespectacled English major.

Later, when the other two huddled in a conversation that excluded us, Junko seized the opportunity to lean in and say, in a confidential whisper:

"Hey, I know what you've been doing."

I didn't like the sound of that, and it must have shown on my face. For one thing, *I* wasn't all that sure what I had been doing for the past eight months since the onset of my breakdown.

"Oh?" I said. "What's that?"

I didn't really want to know, and that must have shown, too. I was still recovering snatches of memory from the previous summer and early fall, the worst period for excessive drinking and pill-popping. At best, my actions were merely embarrassing. At worst...

"No, no," she said, patting my arm. "Nothing bad. What did you think I meant?"

"Well, when I have trouble getting to sleep, I've often imagined my students naked."

"Really? That's nothing."

Her encouragement, augmented by my third beer, formed a dangerous fuel. "I like to imagine ten or so, in a meadow, forming a line, and then they take turns running and leaping over a fence."

"Ah-hah..."

"But—sorry, what were you going to say?"

"Oh. I just wanted to tell you that I know what you've been doing all these years. For your students, I mean."

"For students?"

"For the ones like us who want to study abroad especially. How hard you work to let us study abroad."

"Oh. That."

"No other teacher does what you do. Nobody."

"Gee. Thanks."

"No, it's not just talk. I really mean it. These guys feel the same way. That's why we invited you."

So I went home from that party feeling somewhat friskier than I had in some time, albeit with the knowledge that depression was still lurking somewhere deep. Certainly, international events were not likely to cheer me up in the dawning year...

January 20, 2001: George W. Bush was sworn in as 43rd president of the United States.

...and it was unlikely that I would ever see Junko again. So if I was ever to whip my demons into a turnbuckle once and for all, someone would have to appear to provide fresh distractions and reboot my mindset.

A savior, as it were.

Ahh Yuu Ok-kei?

Let the woman learn in silence with all subjection.

—*1 Timothy 2:11*

Hwat-oh eezu dissu? (What is this?)
That is my ass.
Ahh yuu ok-key? (Are you okay?)
Well, you tell me.

—First contact with Shojo M, April 2001

I certainly wanted to *believe* that I was okay—that my left butt-cheek was making a favorable impression—but after all, who am I to judge the tactile sensations experienced by an eighteen-year-old Japanese freshman girl fondling the flesh of her forty-five-year-old American teacher on the first day of class? I am nobody, that's who. (Indeed, this same freshman girl would interrupt a lesson a few months later to inform me, and the class, "Yuu ahh nasshin-gu" [You are nothing]).

But on that later occasion, she would not be fondling my buttock through the fabric of my JC Penney-bought khaki trousers as she was now, while I eagerly awaited a verdict. I suppose it came down to how much basis for comparative judgment she had accumulated in her eighteen years. (Ah, Comparative Judgment! My ancient, implacable foe!)

On the one hand, she was a bumpkin from a rural province who had just entered a university founded by puritanical Protestants. Few if any of her freshman female peers could claim any expertise, evaluating-the-firmness-of-middle-aged-white-fellows'-buttcheeks-wise. On the other, she was unusually tarted up for a girl on her first day of college. The eyes in particular suggested that an ungallant porn stud who ejaculates mascara had had his way with her that morning.

Was I *ok-key* on Opening Day, April 2001? I was less than a year removed from a breakdown. I believe I've already promised not to bore you with said breakdown's details, but you can probably guess that it involves a guy standing on a station platform in the rain with a comical look on his face because his insides have been kicked out, as these things are wont to do.

And then she walks in. Of all the classrooms in all the universities in all the world, she walks into mine. The little red-haired girl with the scratchy sing-song voice way down in Springsteen range and an ineptitude in English pronunciation that she had no intention of overcoming.

I had seated the freshmen in random pairs and given them assorted get-acquainted questions to ask each other in English while I circulated and monitored, as per custom. But Madoka quickly grew bored with her partner, the pasty-faced (and, as I would later learn, aerobically dull) Kisaburo Baba, so that any remotely appealing object passing by at eye level—a dust mote, say, or my left buttock—was apt to prove an irresistible distraction.

"Have you and your partner finished all the questions?" I asked.

"Hwat-oh eezu *dissu*?" (What is *this*?) she repeated, poking at my pocket this time.

"Oh, *that*? It is my wallet."

"Eh??"

"Wal…let. See?"

"Ah! Geebu me mah-neh!" (Give me money!)

"No!" I said, swiftly withdrawing the object from grabbing range. "Well, not yet."

It's going to be an interesting year with this girl, I thought to myself. Heavenly? Maybe. Hellish? Possibly. Mundane? Not a chance.

Uncomfortable with silence, she said: "Yuu-ah no-zu ho-ru-zu ahh beri puritty." (Your nose-holes are very pretty.)

— ¤ —

I thought about returning the compliment but felt it a bit early in our acquaintance for a frank exchange of views on the aesthetics of each other's orifices. I'm just old-fashioned that way, you see.

I suppose I could have paid tribute to her short, swirly hair, the hue of orangutan fur; or her ludicrously lush fake eyelashes. I might have remarked on her eyeliner, applied that morning (and every other morning of her freshman year) in a quantity sufficient to handwrite the constitution of an emerging nation. Anyway, the moment passed.

After class, I retreated apace to the English teachers' preparation room, happy to still have body and finances together, where I related the extraordinary events of the period to a simpatico younger colleague. "Could you send her to me?" he asked.

This was not a rhetorical question: The first week of April was an observation period, at the end of which a number of students would be moved to levels better suited to their proficiency. I surprised myself with the force of my reaction.

"I wouldn't give you Madoka for every girl in your class," I said.

— ¤ —

First compulsory email from Madoka:

Hi, Muggins!

Now I introduce myself. Are you okay? Today, I talk you about my high school life, school is build the middle of the field and pear orchard. There is much kind of vegetables, such as the leek, Japanese radish, broccoli, nappa, and so on...

I love my school days, but I don't like our teachers. They broke our dream, because they ignored our opinion. But there are present [pleasant?] times, I belonged to domestic science club, the member of it is under 10 people... but we are very very good friends. Last summer, we drank all night long in midnight. we were running the road with singing songs a loud voice. And when I was a third-year high school student, I was the leader of a cheer group of an athletic festival. Then and every one wore "yukata" except for me, and I put on a wig of an Afro, and we danced with PinkLady's song. we had very interesting time, It is my impressive memory of summer time...

—□—

Favorite freshwoman Madoka called me up on Thursday and invited herself over with her cuter friend Tomiko plus a couple of other girls from that class, Tomomi and Yui. They stayed just long enough to eat over 5000 yen of pizza, but there is the promise of more hilarity to come, now that they know where I live.

This Madoka is a truck-load of fun, though. She organized a drinking party last night through sheer force of will—actually just by decreeing offhand one day in class that we would have a party. Practically everybody showed up. I bought flowers for her. She rubbed my head and every part of me that's legal. She repeatedly clutched and squeezed Miya Nojiri's breasts, an event that I repeatedly tried and failed to capture on film. The party was the second violation in a week of my no-drinking-in-May policy, but well worth the cost in brain cells and extra money.

My only Madoka-based regret is that I could not dine with her at the Freshmen Camp, which was conveniently held in a hotel just across the street from Yamashita Park this year. I cleverly timed my entrance just before the buffet, only to be told by a sophomore that if I entered the hall, I would immediately be whisked away to a long and tedious professors-only party. Characteristically, I fled after having spent all of five minutes at the "camp." I never got to see Madoka in her allegedly sexy dress.

May 2001

In a tactic borrowed from the seedier new religions, the IR faculty held a "freshman camp" a month into the academic year, during which they spirited the new IR majors to a hotel somewhere for two days of indoctrination. The first such camp, held the previous year, had quickly devolved into a bacchanal owing to vending machines throughout the hotel that dispensed alcoholic beverages.

This time, the faculty took extreme measures to keep freshmen and alcohol apart, even unto posting guards at the hotel exits. Madoka, not to be denied, led a team of commandoes[*] down several flights of fire escape and over a ten-foot concrete wall, then back to their rooms laden with liquor. Presumably, she changed clothes for this, though I prefer to imagine her doing it in the same slinky gown that she wore for the banquet, giving her a Bond Girl vibe.[†]

Whatever she wore, I couldn't have been prouder if I were her Pop.

—◻—

Second compulsory email from Madoka:

---

[*] Very possibly including the pluperfectly nondescript Kisaburo Baba, a beige presence easily molded to her will.

[†] She would have been the double-crossing type Bond Girl who gets killed in spectacular fashion during the climactic demolition-of-villain's-lair sequence, never the easily seduced naïf that falls prey in Act I to a silly flying hat or some such.

Today is twenty in June. Yesterday, I went to your house with Yui in night. First, it was raining hard, so I try not to your house, but it stopped raining, we can go your house and we can spend precious time. I'm sorry not only to sleep but also I obstruct to you taught for Yui. She is nice girl. She is so wonderful. Tomiko and I often say that today, Yui gave pleasure for us. She is certainly our idol. But her house is little dirty, noisy, and offensive.

By the way, now I'm telling you my favorite foods, so please give me these foods. I like Udon, Yakisoba, kimchi, Chinese noodle in soup, and especially I like an eggplant. This is very good taste and easy to cook any way. So I eat it one or two time in a week.

Next, I told you what I think these days. Hmmm… I told you that there is a [river] bank in front of my house, didn't you? So these days, many young people did fire work and I heard they're voice as very exciting. I want to do such a thing in near days. Let's do fire work and go to sea with English Class member in summer. Summer is best season to enjoy anything; I feel everything so exciting and funny only in summer. How do you spend in every summer? Please tell me in your replay. OK see you.

The visit to my apartment by Madoka and two female friends was not entirely social. They had been assigned by the teacher of another class to translate a news article from English to Japanese, and Madoka insisted that I help them cheat. Her belly full of pizza, she further insisted that Yui and Tomiko finish debriefing me on her behalf while she unrolled my futon and went to sleep.

When she awoke, I implied that a bit of physical intimacy might be suitable compensation for the two unbilled hours of my time. She squinted at my bald pate, coated with a patina of sweat owing to humidity and the hours of concentration, and proceeded to wipe it with a few of the pore-cleansing pads found in the utility belts of all young Japanese ladies.

She's magnificent. No thought, no notion, no matter how ludicrous or meaningless, ever appears in the depths of her brain without immediately bubbling up to the surface and getting expressed out loud, in absurd katakana *English.*

June 2001

—◻—

Hello!I'm Madoka Wada. Please call me. I want to go Muggins house.

I quickly and enthusiastically replied that I would treat her to pizza and asked for particulars.

OH ! GORO AND SHIORI SAIED TO WANT GO YOU'RE HOUSE,AND I THINK THAT HIDEO DOESN'T EAT DINNER EVERYDAY. SO I WANT TO TAKE HIM WITH US. ARE YOU OK ? I'M LOOKING FORWARD THE DAY. SEE YOU TOMORROW. MADOKA

In a blitzkrieg social offensive, she had made the class her own; I was merely allowed to stand in front of the room as a figurehead, like the Queen opening Parliament.

If there were ever to be any sexual activity between us, I was certain, it would be initiated by her and be cruel. My best-case scenario would involve getting trussed in leather with a red ball in my mouth and locked inside a trunk; more likely, there would be peeing on my chest. Even so, I remained hopeful that I would be able to start masturbating to her once the weather got warmer and I could better comprehend her assets.

She never really fielded her team in NU's competitive Cleavage League, but did possess an array of sleeveless shirts and blouses. "Oh, God," I hissed to Tomiko one day as Madoka swaggered into the room late, "look at that." But Tomiko was unimpressed, dismissing Madoka's bare arms as "mannish."

—◻—

133

The annual summer fireworks display at Yokohama's Yamashita Park was always a BFD for the Nangaku hoi polloi.

Yesterday was fireworks at Yamashita Park. After a year off for mental crackup, I was back—this time as sole leader of a contingent of 16 freshmen. Actually, Madoka was supposed to be my co-leader, but she abandoned me at the last minute. I had to call on Goro Watanabe, a poor substitute. "Ahhhh, Mag-gyoon!" cried Goro when I contacted him on his cell phone.

We got to the park by 3:30 and staked our claim, and I was left to fry in the sun while Goro rounded everybody else up. Though I messed up a few things, I was on the whole a surprisingly good leader, and we even had a good time at Watami afterward...

Madoka showed up only for the last 20 minutes of fireworks and the drinking. I tried to express my disappointment, but she seems invulnerable to snubbing. Shiori Taniguchi looked great in her tiny little summer top...

July 2001

Madoka did not have peers per se, nor friends, nor even followers, so much as she had minions. Her two most prominent satellites were Tomiko, who possessed the fawn-like eyes and flowing locks and pubescent shape that drove freshman boys wild, and Shiori, an unfailingly cheerful and rosy-cheeked cherub with a pixie cut. The plain and studious Yui had made a fourth for a while, but faded toward the end of the first semester once she discerned that Madoka was only using her as a homework service.

On the male side of the ledger, the only notable players were Goro and Hee-DAY-yoh, which suited me fine, as neither posed a credible threat. They were scarcely more substantial than Kisaburo Baba, that dictionary definition of a nonentity.* Both were heirs to

---

* I once toyed with the idea of putting a black-framed mugshot of him on my website with the caption "In Loving Memory of Kisaburo Baba, 1982-2001" just to see how many people would casually assume he was dead, even as he continued coming to class every day. That's how thin a shadow Kisaburo cast. I didn't follow through, though; it just seemed like far too much effort to expend on the likes of Kisaburo Baba.

a long NU tradition of male comic relief characters whom NU females regarded as perhaps even less likely mates than me.

Goro looked and behaved like a journeyman actor's tossed-off interpretation of the Joker, somewhere in the Cesar Romero-to-Jack Nicholson continuum. Instead of a snide "Ahhhh, Batman and the Boy Blunder!" he unfailingly greeted me with "Ahhhh, Mag-*gyoon*!" his best shot at pronouncing my name.

Less sunny was the tall, anorexic Hideo. It was his misfortune that Kintetsu Buffaloes pitcher Hideo Nomo had made his historic leap to the US major leagues a few years earlier, inspiring a "Banana Boat Song" parody ("Hee-*DAY*-yoh! Hee-*DAY*-*YAY*-*YAY*-yoh!") and thus making it inevitable that any boy of the same name would be called Hee-*DAY*-yoh, and by summer of his freshman year, the habit had become so ingrained that I even called him Hee-*DAY*-yoh when I was annoyed with him, which was most of the time.

So I had looked forward to organizing the aforementioned fireworks-cum-drinking outing together with Madoka, sure to be a memorable bonding experience for us, but ended up partnering with Goro instead. Upon his arrival at the park, I gave him the equivalent of fifty dollars to purchase soft drinks and snacks for all the people expected to come. He returned ninety minutes later with a single bag of potato chips and no change.

—▫—

"There's this freshman girl that I really like who sometimes comes to visit me," I wrote to an alumnus. "I'm spending a lot of money on her."

"Sounds like *enjo kosai*," he noted in his terse reply, referring to the very same seedy "compensated dating" practice that had once sparked a tense showdown between Great Nangaku Woman Honami Torihata and me.

Was it *enjo kosai*? I sat down in early autumn and toted up all the *enjo*—compensation—that I had laid out in the form of drinks, pizzas, magical potato chips and so forth. It came to about three hundred fifty yankee dollahs.

Then I added up all the *kosai*—physical services that Madoka had rendered. It amounted to one incidence of blotting sweat from my head with absorbent paper and occasional outbreaks of buttocks-squeezing.

I promptly mailed these results to the cheeky alumnus and, for good measure, posted them on my website.

—◻—

I had an amusing dinner at Barmyan with Madoka, as planned, last Monday, but she made sure there were plenty of other people with us: Hee-DAY-yoh, Tomiko, and her high school friend Mana.

July 2001

That Madoka was able to so nearly monopolize my attention for an entire spring semester and summer vacation was a feat that needs to be put into context. Through some bureaucratic blunder, International Relations had admitted a huge freshman cohort that year, some one hundred thirty percent of the quota. The usual seven-to-three gender ratio prevailed, meaning that Madoka had some two hundred and sixty rivals for my affection just within her own entering class.

On top of that, the assorted semipro models and hard-drinkin' good-time broads who had entered the previous year were still very much in their prime and open to suggestions for get-togethers. An actual ex-girlfriend was still on the premises, if seldom glimpsed. And of course, there were the other NU majors with their exotically nippleless women, if one were up for that sort of thing. The mind reels.

—◻—

In my other freshman English class, to give but one example, there was a girl named Asami, whose picture I had fallen in love with before classes even began. During the orientation week in early April, I detached the mugshot from her Placement Test questionnaire so that I could carry it around in my breast pocket and show it to any and all IR boys that I encountered.

"Hi. Want to see a picture of a pretty freshman girl who'll be in my class? Check her out."

"*Ii nahh!*" (Roughly "Aw, man!" or "I envy you!")

"I'll be meeting Asami four times a week. But you'll probably never meet her!"

"*Ii nahh!*"

Later, Asami would inform me via her email journal that both of her parents had been killed in a traffic accident just a few years earlier.

At the same time that I had been falling to pieces over a relationship gone bad, recently orphaned Asami was pulling herself together for university entrance exams. While I spent large chunks of 2001 whining into my pillow and waiting to see my psychiatrist and zoning out on meds, she cheerfully went about the business of racking up A's.*

—¤—

Madoka liked to invent games. Prior to summer vacation, she described one that we would play at the beach during a trip that never materialized:

---

* And when news came later that year that jetliners were slamming into skyscrapers in New York City—a story that broke shortly after ten p.m. in Japan—Asami was the first person to contact me that long, eerie night. "What will follow?" she asked.

Here was my chance to play Responsible Adult and send her to bed with some soothing bromide. Instead, I predicted dire military and economic consequences, and confessed to being frightened.

"Yuu suweemu een zah shee. Den *wee* suweemu een zah shee. Den wee kyatchi yuu."

(You swim in the sea. Then *we* swim in the sea. Then we catch you.)

The name of this game, I was informed, was "Catch Muggins."

Almost unconsciously, we collaborated to craft a game called "Imperial Family," which was played every week after class on Tuesday. Our second-floor classroom on that day was adjacent to a large outdoor patio that resembled the balcony from which the emperor and his extended family waved to visitors during ceremonies marking the New Year and the emperor's birthday. Madoka and I played the imperial couple, with Tomiko and Shiori and whoever else was handy fleshing out the clan as assorted princesses. The object was to get our loyal subjects—aka the weary masses trudging to class below us—to wave back.

Even when not devising games, Madoka and her pretty underlings managed to inspire their creation. After class one morning, Goro and Hee-DAY-yoh and I entered into a spontaneous competition to see who could first achieve a standing vertical jump onto one of the classroom desks. In our quest for the girls' attention, however, we were badly outclassed by their cell phones, which was just as well, as I barked a shin badly on my last attempt. This is as good a time as any, I suppose to remind readers that I was then forty-six years old.

—◻—

It took the considerable power of Shojo M to snap me out of [a post-birthday funk]. *She informed me that she would be coming over on Tuesday to celebrate Chohei Kim's birthday. There were five of them, and I took it in the ass on the pizza bill, but it was well worth it. Madoka bitched at and flirted with me by turns, insisted on melting Hershey bars to make chocolate popcorn and in the process of doing so nearly blew up my microwave.*

October 2001

Around this time, I created a dedicated page on my website for her. All photos of Madoka uploaded there would include a raccoon-style bandit mask photoshopped over her face for "privacy." I gave her the cover name Shojo M, "Girl M."* An updatable list of her more illustrious quotes and the ongoing *enjo* vs. *kosai* tabulation were among the more popular features.

Alas, before that page was ready to be launched, our relationship, like most radioactive substances when left lying around without adult supervision, began to degrade. By the middle of fall semester, she was taking advantage of my adoration to misbehave in class, spurring the easily spurred Goro into noisy conversation while I was trying to explain the safe rules of essay organization, for example.

This led to the writing and passing of stern notes, and when that didn't work, trying to get her to sit down for a heart-to-heart during lunch hour. She listened to me impatiently for about thirty seconds, then shut me down to take a phone call, leaving me shaking in rage. Shaking, I tell you.

In retrospect, Shojo M's classroom behavior probably had not grown any more outrageous over time. This, after all, was a girl who had clutched my butt-cheek and complimented my nostrils on the first day of class. The breakdown was probably equal parts exhaustion of my capacity for indulgence and a decision to go off my meds without my doctor's consent.

In any event, our class headed toward the holidays in a decidedly dour mood.

— ¤ —

Friday, December 21, was the last day of regular class before the holiday break, but the university had designated some days during

---

* The Japanese police were fond of this type of designation for minors embroiled in crimes.

the last week of December for makeup classes. Dodgy mental health notwithstanding, I had not canceled any classes that semester; but I scheduled a full day of extra classes for the 24th simply because so many of my students had fallen so woefully behind in their work that they would not be able to pass their required English courses if left to their own devices.

So it would be an invitation-only affair. Indeed, I printed up actual invitation cards, using one of those cursive fonts: *You are cordially invited to attend a full day of tedious extra assignments*, and so on and so forth, replete with Christmassy clip-art. In the preceding week I had doled them out, leaving behind me a trail of delayed-reaction whines and groans as the recipients digested the contents.

My journal entries from this period make much of my tremendous generosity, devotion to duty, and self-sacrifice in arranging this opportunity for the slackers to improve their fate. Most of my colleagues, I felt (and not without reason), would simply have let all of them fail. In retrospect, however, I suspect that my primary motivation was to avoid being alone at Christmas.

—◻—

Shojo M was not invited; she was too crafty at gaming my grading system and thus not endangered. Nor was Kisaburo Baba, simply too boring to be a bad student. Of course, Goro was summoned, as was Hee-DAY-yoh.

They were told to arrive in the computer classroom by nine a.m., so of course most of them trickled in after ten. I had prepared a customized task sheet for each failer: the miscreant was to remain in the room until he or she had knocked off a sufficient number of items to justify my giving a passing grade.

The largest contingent in the room consisted of those failing Writing, and each of them was given one major assignment to complete: a typed, five-paragraph persuasive essay on the theme "Why I Deserve to Get Credits in Spite of Being a Lazy and Worthless Human Being."

In typically Japanese fashion, nobody visibly bristled at the insult and only one writer, his name long forgotten, took umbrage in his essay. The first paragraph of the body, grammatically cleaned up, went something like this:

First of all, I'm not a worthless human being. And I don't think I'm lazy, either. All right, I couldn't do some of the assignments, but that's because I have my part-time job five nights a week and my parents don't give me any allowance. If you think I'm lazy, I can't do anything about that, but you have no right to call me a worthless human being!

I let him go.

Goro, as was his wont, cheerfully misunderstood the assignment and wrote five paragraphs of giddy off-topic gibberish. I put him through a couple of revisions until the logic of the thing fell short of total insanity and then dismissed him, too. By mid-afternoon, Hee-DAY-yoh and a girl called Maki were the only stragglers.

As I peered over his shoulder at a shimmering blank Word document, Hee-DAY-yoh and I had this exchange:

Hee-DAY-yoh: I'm going home to Hokkaido tonight. My flight leaves Haneda Airport at six-thirty.

Me: Fuck you, Hee-DAY-yoh. You can leave when you finish a perfect essay.

Hee-DAY-yoh: I just want to be with my family.

Me: Bah!

Hee-DAY-yoh: But…it's Christmas Eve, Mr. Muggins!

All right, memory may have fogged some of the details, but that was the gist of our exchange. The thing that Hee-DAY-yoh produced was not on topic, not five paragraphs, and not technically an essay, but if held at arm's length and scanned peripherally while squinting, it passed for one. He was allowed to fly to the bosom of his family.

The afternoon wore on; the sky blackened over the gray, dead grass outside the windows. Maki continued to struggle earnestly with her essay.

—□—

Maki was nineteen going on twelve. The Japanese adult video industry, always on the lookout for "legal" girls who can pass as virginal jailbait, would have clasped her to its seedy bosom, but it was hard to imagine Maki returning the favor, and not only because she had no bosom.

She was elfin, with the helmet-like 'do of junior high school girls who like sports way more than hair care, and she sat through every class with an expression that suggested that she expected me to punch her in the face at any moment.

Her work had been consistently awful all year. She did not join class social events, which was perhaps just as well. In class, I could never pair her with Shojo M for conversation practice for fear that the latter, praying mantis-like, would actually devour Maki's head. Most often, I would saddle her with the inconsequential Baba and ignore them both.

I kept my distance from her that December day, occasionally stealing a glance at her pouty, gender-bender-manga face bathed in the cathode-ray glow of the boxy Fujitsu PC monitor, until she finally printed out her essay and presented it to me.

The corrected version, as reconstructed from memory:

I am sorry to trouble you by taking so long to write my essay.

I don't have any reason why I should get credits. I know that my assignments are not good. The class is very difficult for me.

At the beginning of the year, Muggins said to me maybe I should move to Level 1 class because Level 2 will be too difficult for me. To tell the truth, I also thought it's too difficult for me. But I wanted to stay in Level 2 because Level 2 is Muggins's class. Everyone in International Relations says Muggins is the best teacher. And I think so, too. I can't understand the class well, but I enjoy the class, and I learn English in this class. Muggins teaches us so earnestly and kindly.

I'm sorry that I make trouble for Muggins. I'm lazy sometimes. I will work harder from now on. Thank you for this chance to raise up my grade. I will not disappoint Muggins anymore. Then, Muggins, take care to rest in this vacation and don't catch a cold. Muggins doesn't look fine recently, so I worry.

I thank you from the bottom of my heart and Merry Christmas.

I corrected Maki's errors, added a short note, and sent her home; then headed for my own dark, drafty abode to cry into my Christmas beer alone while contemplating the decent and committed albeit oversexed educator that I may once have been, and might, with some modicum of self-discipline, yet again become.

— ¤ —

Shojo M. went back into the hospital with her throat problems. She missed the test of English 4 as well as the debut of her Tribute Page on my website.

January 2002

Fortunately, she emerged from the hospital just in time for the last day of class, a day traditionally devoted to a brief give-back of the final exam followed by non-alcohol-fueled merriment such as arm-wrestling for bonus points. Shojo M produced snacks and soft drinks for an in-class party, perhaps using the phantom funds that had evaporated in Goro's hands back on Fireworks Day.

"Ahh yuu ok-kay? Hwat-to doo yoo wan-to?" she asked me.

She mangled English with such verve and confidence that you sometimes felt that *you* were the one talking funny.

"Go over there and molest Miya while I take pictures," I replied.

"Ok-*kay!*"

All my differences with her were thus smoothed over on this, the last occasion when we would meet in class as teacher and student. For my part, I was not sad, for the death of our student-teacher relationship gave birth to so many possibilities.

—◻—

There was a party a week ago for Madoka's class. We had okonomi-yaki near Yokohama Station. I drank too much and paid too much, but I had a great time fooling around with the boys. Goro told me he yearned to take the insanely monogamous Tomiko to Hawaii. I launched a paper airplane at the girls' table offering to take whoever caught it to Hawaii. Unfortunately, it was caught by the singularly uninteresting (and unaccountably boyfriended) Airi Onda.

I made Sho Saito give me a massage in order to cement his C grade, moaning in orgasmic pleasure all along. Tomiko translated part of the conversation at the next table in which Miya Nojiri griped that her ex-boyfriend liked to bite her on the ass. Shojo M herself got two phone calls from Akio Iida at the party. I grabbed the phone and told him I'd castrate him with scissors if I had the chance. Madoka told me that Shiori is still a virgin. I invited Shiori to Hawaii.

February 2002

Careful readers will remember this Akio as the helpless lad upon whom I had bestowed exhaustive advice on how to snare an NU woman. Suddenly, he was Madoka's boyfriend.

And thus, the whirligig of time brings in his revenges.

—◻—

April 2002: Year Two of the Shojo M. Era Dawns

Sexy freshman babes Kiko Kogawa and Izumi Hatayama blew me kisses the other day. On Shojo M's birthday yesterday, I gave her chocolate and a suggestive card. Spring is in the air...

A Few Weeks Later

The next night I came home to get a message on my machine from Madoka. She had shown up on my doorstep and was calling from her cell phone. She appeared to be alone... I suppose she just wanted to show me her new car that she's so damned proud of, but, having broken up with Akio Iida, perhaps she had something else to show as well...

May

The week began with Madoka trying to corner me for some sort of actual, sincere talk. She seems to be wondering whether or not she ought to drop out of school altogether. We never did hook up for the talk, though.

July

The butthole-checking guy [i.e., technician administering my colonoscopy] *was as inept as he appeared. He bailed out a third of the way through and called in his* [supervisor], *who was chatty and informative, and relatively painless.*

My ass was declared a living national treasure by the chief of butthole-ology, and I cheerfully reported the same to Madoka via cell. I would be able to attend her class's party the next night after all.

A Few Days Later

Fatigue, age, a deep anal probing in the medical sense plus an equally aggressive reaming in the career sense combined to make me a rather drippy guest at the sophomore party Friday night.

I vowed to drink little, behave myself, and come home early. I almost pulled it off. True, I did kiss Goro on the lips to celebrate his consuming a raw garlic bulb. And I flirted shamelessly with the virginally blushing Shiori Taniguchi. And I asked Kisaburo Baba, apropos of nothing, what the largest object he had ever stuck up his butt was. But otherwise, I had been a model citizen.

I paid my now-obligatory 10,000 yen and tried to flee, but was waylaid by a hysterical and prat-falling Tomiko. It seems I had missed the point of the whole party. This was Madoka and Miya's fond farewell to Nangaku. There was a ceremony to follow, replete with speeches and the passing of bouquets. Tomiko broke down in tears in the midst of her conned speech in honor of her friend Madoka. Madoka showed no emotion, but I was moved.

Madoka received her bouquet in a denim midi and Green Bay Packers t-shirt. Miya went with jeans and an uncharacteristically demure long-sleeve white blouse, perhaps in hopes of discouraging Madoka from randomly mauling her large, full bosoms, as was her wont.

Madoka plans to go to Australia on "working holiday." I weep for Australia…and a little for myself.

But Shojo M would be okay wherever she went. The mind naturally flowed backward to that first fateful encounter, and her first question, so often repeated thereafter: *Ahh yuu ok-key?*

Maybe I was. Just maybe I finally was, thanks in no small part to the little red-haired girl.

Five Disagreeable Things I Did Because NU Chicks Made Me

There is a difference between being whipped and being a gentleman.

— Anonymous

Every morning since 1996, I have sipped my coffee from an ancient white mug. At least I still think of it as white. Its interior is now ringed with brown striations that have bonded at a molecular level with the ceramic. Finishing off the morning coffee is like peering into the toilet in the basement of a frat house populated by hard-drinking chipmunks.

The mug's exterior sports some sort of chocolaty illustration identifiable only by the caption under it: *Joe Bruin 1996*. No longer recognizable as a bear, it has faded and blurred to the point where it now looks as if the UCLA mascot is a thick, corn-flecked turd with a jaunty name.

This cup would not be a very appetizing vessel with which to begin a day but for the fact that it was given to me by an NU girl. It expresses her gratitude for my enabling her to spend the 1995-96 academic year studying in California.

My journal makes no mention of the giver. It doesn't matter, really. All that matters is that an NU girl picked up this item in a campus store, held it in her hand, contemplated it with her eye, conceived the notion that "Muggins might like this" with her mind, and then brought it halfway around the world to give to me,* and that knowledge makes the coffee, freeze-dried though it is, go down smoother. I have used it for nearly nineteen years at this writing and will continue to do so until either it falls apart or I do. Voluntarily parting with a toe or two would be easier than parting with an artifact of an NU woman's affection.

There was nothing an NU chick could give me that I would not treasure and use, no matter how useless or ludicrous, nor were there many things that I would not do if they asked me to—not just Shojo M, but pretty much the lot of them. I'm that romantic, and that pathetic.

A random sampling:

1. Handing out leaflets in the dead of winter

Later that day, I had a date with Toko in Harajuku at her request. The excuse for getting together was to support a photo exhibit organized by IR seniors in support of Kobe earthquake victims. As only she can, she got me to stand on a busy Harajuku street and hand out leaflets with her. That hour or so of standing still in the late-winter chill may well have been instrumental to the crushing flu that attacked me a few days later. If so, I guess it was worth it after all.

March 1995

Toying with my immune system, like toying with my heart, was something of a pastime for NU women, as the next item confirms.

2. Chika's damn outdoor Xmas pageant

On Tuesday, Hogan and I put up with Chika's damn outdoor Xmas

---

* To be sure, the reality was likely more along the lines of *Holy crap, my flight leaves tomorrow and I forgot to buy souvenirs for the lesser people! I'll just shovel a bunch of this dreck into the basket and sort it out when I get back.* But let's not spoil the mood, shall we?

pageant. Hogan was a Wise Man and therefore got to wear shoes. It was a so-called "guerilla performance" for people passing by the chapel on their way to the taxi stand, but no one stopped to see us. Indeed, the light was so dim by then, no one could see us if they tried. It was absurd.

December 2001

"My friends and I will perform a Christmas pageant," apple-cheeked chick Chika chirped one chilly November day. "Will you appear in it?"

Chika was just as I remembered her from freshman English class: ivory-soap-complected and still a stranger to any form of cosmetic. The long, slightly kinky, jet-black hair, parted in the middle, suggested an Indian maiden from a primary school Thanksgiving play; indeed, she even braided it on occasion. Her eyebrows remained as God has designed them.

When she stripped out of her Puritanical clothes, as she would later do, right there in the multi-purpose room next to the school chapel to get into her angel costume for the pageant, it seemed to us as if some mad and naughty scientist had transplanted the head of an eleven-year-old tomboy onto the body of a porn star.

That inspiring display was still a good month away as Chika and I chatted in front of the library. Even with her body still an undiscovered country, Chika commanded a formidable degree of cuteness. The utterance "Will you appear in my Christmas pageant?" from such a personage was automatically processed by middle-aged male ears into *You will appear in my Christmas pageant*. All I could do was ask for particulars.

It would be a nativity play, she said, to be performed outdoors in front of the chapel in the late afternoon of a December day just as students were sure to be filing past that edifice on the way home after fourth-period class. The other participants would be her mates in the Chapel-sponsored Christian club and Mr. Hogan, another English teacher. I was to be Shepherd Number Two.

"Shepherd Number Two? Really? What about Hogan?"

"He will be a wise man."

I wasn't about to take that. I was in a no-beard phase at the time, and, being hairless on both the northern and southern hemispheres of my head, put my name forward for a more central role.

"No. We don't need a baby Jesus."

"More people will stop and watch if there's an English teacher in a diaper," I pleaded.

"Oh, do you think so?"

—◻—

I had theretofore never actively explored my own feelings on this whole publicity-value-of-a-diaper-clad-teacher issue, and so was rather surprised at the intensity with which I held this view. But Chika was equally immovable. The baby Jesus would be portrayed symbolically by a spray of artificial lilies. So I would have to content myself with playing second fiddle to Hogan and third fiddle to a dainty clump of plastic. As I said, Chika possessed a formidable cuteness.

Of course, the casting slight—augmented though it was by the shimmering crimson robe that Wise Man Hogan was supplied with as juxtaposed with the wrinkled white bedsheet that I got—was quickly forgotten when Hogan and I got an eyeful of Chika's unsuspected curves in the changing room. And, lo, the angel of the Lord came upon us, and the glory of Chika's protuberant hooters shone round about us: and we were sore afraid.

And afraid we well should be: for men such as us to allow ourselves impure thoughts of a girl such as her, then in the process of preparing to portray an entity such as that, in such a sanctified place and in such a holy season, was to bring down about thirty-seven distinct flavors of eternal damnation upon our souls. We bravely fantasized forth, nonetheless.

—◻—

During the lone rehearsal that we squeezed in just before the lone performance, it became clear that Chika's concept of a nativity play lacked other essentials besides a convincing Jesus.

We were a cast of six, among whom Chika was our only female. Since she opted to play an angel who delivers the infant Christ, there would be no Virgin Mary. Ergo, no Joseph. It was like arranging a reunion episode of *Friends*, only without the Friends. The orphaned plastic bouquet was to be unceremoniously dumped on a folding chair by the angel while a pair of wise men to the left and a trio of shepherds to the right gesticulated our astonishment.

Astonishment was the only proper reaction to such a tableau. Lord knows it was the expression favored by passers-by who involuntarily glimpsed any part of the spectacle. Instrumental versions of "Silent Night" and "Oh Come, All Ye Faithful" wafted softly but raspily from a too-small cassette player. The wise men and shepherds shuffled in from opposite sides. I noticed for the first time that the wise men were allowed to wear shoes while we shepherds suffered in bare feet out in the December twilight.

Chika then fluttered in wearing a shimmering silk-ish robe that obscured her physique even more than her usual thick sweaters did. Her entrance cued the aforementioned gesticulation. The wise men made do with a series of dignified bows while the kneeling shepherds, callow rustics that we were, reacted to the Angel Chika with slack jaws and a series of bobbing, arm-flailing gestures that suggested overtaxed synchronized swimmers clamoring in unison for life preservers.

Chika then deposited the Holy Corsage, causing us shepherds to prostrate ourselves in awe. Then the non-Hogan wise man stepped forward and broke character to narrate what had happened, on the erroneous assumption that anyone gave a shit.

—◻—

For reasons I could not fathom, Chika and her friends regarded the pageant as a smashing success. As we surreptitiously watched her change back to her terrestrial form, I thought I heard her and her club-mates discussing a most reprehensible notion in Japanese. Then, sure enough:

"Would you mind performing the pageant again here next year?" she asked, apple cheeks all aglow. Hogan and I, trapped in our ageing heterosexual bodies, shrugged why not.

3. Wearing miscellaneous gift-crap

My birthday and the last day of the school year were the two occasions on which I might receive gifts from a class—especially from the IR freshmen taking required English. Year in and year out, successive generations looked me up and down and arrived at the same conclusion: *comical headgear*.

Thus was I given, and in many instances forced to wear for a specified time or distance, the following:

➢ An afro wig

➢ A floppy stocking hat similar to that worn by picture-book icon Waldo, but in a less manly color scheme

➢ Earmuffs fashioned after the head of the Pikachu character from *Pokemon*

➢ A golf cap, although I never golf

➢ A ski mask more suitable for hostage-taking than skiing (I rarely do either)

➢ Playboy bunny ears

➢ Some white, furry abomination in the shape of a top hat

➤ A wig of close-cropped black hair with a bald spot on it (evidently modeled on a Japanese animation character with whom I was not familiar)

➤ Earmuffs fashioned on the head of Miffy, hench-rabbit of Hello Kitty

➤ A rainbow-colored fright wig

Every year I would pluck some such head-warming monstrosity from its packaging and murmur through clenched teeth something along the lines of:

Why, what's this? A rainbow-colored fright wig? Oh…oh, I see! It's because I haven't got any hair, am I right? You want me to keep my head warm in this chilly season? Oh, that's hilarious! How did you come up with something like this? Well, I never… Ha! Ha! Ha! Really, you guys are just too much! Too much…

4. Attending depressing wedding receptions

Willowy Glee Club alumna Masami got married four years after graduation and invited me. I did not perceive it as a slight that I was not invited to the ceremony and main reception, given that it is customary to fork over a cash gift of around three hundred dollars on site on such occasions. No, an invitation to the actual wedding of a former student is something to be looked at with the same attitude one would bring to bear upon a subpoena or a positive paternity test.

Instead, I was to attend the *nijikai*, or second reception, a much less formal and more affordable gathering reserved for persons that the couple actually like.

It was Masami who had emerged as de facto honcho of my

backup singers at the not-especially-ill-fated live concert I had given at a school festival in the throes of my great depression of the early Aughts—even unto recruiting our sound engineer and receptionist, and having matching pink t-shirts bearing my name produced at her own expense*—and it was Masami who had bitch-slapped me into going through with the thing when I tried to slither out of it.

So I could hardly refuse when she called to bitch-slap me once again into giving the kick-off toast at her *nijikai*, even though I was suffering a flurry of headaches that occasionally blurred my vision.

I was happy for Masami, who looked lovely. She really had been very sweet to me during the most difficult of times. But the event saddened me. It was one of those occasional glimpses I get into the world of ordinary people who marry and live with their spouses and have plenty of friends and live normal lives. A normal, boring life looked pretty good to me last night as I staggered half-blind out of that café.

April 2006

5. Translating Asada Girls' presentations

Erstwhile lust objects charged back into my life oh-so-briefly in order to beg for my editing of the reports that they would have to deliver during their study trip to the Philippines.

Yes, there I was, suddenly, across the table from Ruriko as she purred meaningfully at me and arched those Joan Crawford eyebrows. For her part, Toko sat really, really close to me and put her hand on my knee at one point.

December 1995

Like any of its female inhabitants, the Yokohama campus itself

---

* Anyway, the photographic record informs me that the girls wore such shirts, and I was in no condition to coordinate any such thing, so I'm pinning it on Masami.

has a charm and mystique and beauty uniquely its own—and never more so than at seven on a crisp autumn morning, long before any said inhabitants would arrive. Now an early riser might enter by the chapel and enjoy a slow, thoughtful stroll the entire length of the grounds to the International Relations headquarters with no aural disruptions beyond the jaded cawing of the odd crow.

Gazing at the now lifeless alabaster blocks that compose the campus, the stroller can imagine himself touring the lost civilization of the Anasazi. And might not these slowly twisting wisps of mist be the lingering spirits of that mysterious race? And might not—

"Muhhh-ginnnnnssssss!!"

Sweet bleeding paperboy of Moses, *what was that?* This ungodly cry that conjures up a whiff of nostalgia and the rusty taste of terror at the same time... Could it be?

"Muhhh-ginnnnnssssss!! Wait!"

Yes, it could be, and it is: Toko, entering campus from a different angle. Instinct kicks in, and I flee across the bridge. My assailant takes this as a form of play: the piercing shriek of her laughter and her flat, pounding footfalls scatter the crows.

"Muh-muh-muhgins!! Sto-sto-stop!" she seems to stutter, as her caterwauls carom off the buildings that wall us in. I must obey, having run out of campus. We are now in the quad, scene of the crime where Toko once bullied me into square-dancing at high noon to a tom-tom.

And that, in a nutshell, is how I got the pro bono report-editing contract.

—□—

Every winter, the juniors in Professor Asada's two-year research seminar in development economics embarked on a study trip to a couple of Southeast Asian nations. There, they presented ten-page research papers and gave presentations based on them as a basis for discussion with local students—all of which had to be done in

English.

To select the dozen or so finalists who would gain admission to his popular seminar, Professor Asada would submit each applicant to an intense one-on-one interview aimed at gauging his or her econ IQ and work ethic; then, he would pretty much just select the girls who gave him the biggest and purplest erections.* He would always chuck in a random male applicant or two in the deluded belief that this covered his tracks. Of course Asada had admitted my album-making conspirators Toko and Ruriko. He and I had similar tastes, after all.

Along about the sixth week of seminar class with the new members, the professor would suddenly be seized by the epiphany that his students possessed neither knowledge of development economics nor the desire to obtain it. This would never fail to astonish him.

His thoughts would then bend toward his arch-nemesis Professor Truong, lurking down there in Ho Chi Minh City with his crack troop of lean and hungry scholars, just waiting to humiliate him and his retinue of pretty idiots yet again when the two groups met for their colloquium.

Down these dark alleyways would his thoughts meander until a gleaming slice of especially fetching cleavage would knock all concerns about the study trip out of his mind; soon it would be too late to deal sensibly with the problem, at which point he would conclude, "Better lay a honey trap for Muggins."†

—◻—

The first time I had ever seen him, at a reception for visiting

---

* I imagined him at his desk, peering intently into a mugshot for five seconds, then glancing down to assess his purplitude, then jotting a note, then flipping to the next mugshot…

† All conjecture, mind you.

faculty, he was holding a cigarette in one hand and a cocktail in the other, while still managing to use both arms to pin a blonde American English teacher into a corner.

He was already graying by then, but one could see the dashing young lion he once had been, what with his taut build and confident stride and wavy mane. On the annual trips to the tropics, he liked to take his students to a beach, mainly for the chance to assess them, of course, but also to flash his own form in a very small Speedo. Accounts varied as to whether he was still able to pull off this fashion statement in his fifties, by which time the smoking and drinking was beginning to take a toll.

Like a lot of seminar professors, he liked to lead his group to one of the bar-restaurants near the local train station for refreshments after class. In addition to drinking and smoking, he enjoyed sliding a hand up and down the back of his neighbor now and then.*

—◻—

"What is this ODA?" I asked, clicking a pencil against the cathode-ray computer screen.

"I don't know. Ruriko, what is ODA?"

Ruriko didn't know either, but started to look it up.

"Okay, and you say here that the ODA to the Philippines increased during the Eighties."

"Yes."

"But *here*, you say just the opposite—that it *decreased* in the Eighties."

"Yes."

"Well, which is it? Did it increase, or decrease?"

"Yes."

---

* I considered him not a role model, but something on the order of a stalking horse, or maybe the canary in my coal mine, or maybe my stalking canary—one of those things. Anyway, so long as no disciplinary action befell Asada, I figured I was safe.

"Ahhhhhh!!"

And so it went, page by bloody page, line by agonizing line, clause by tortured clause. Somehow, by triangulating the original Japanese version of the paper, the butchered English draft, and charades, we were able to craft language that expressed the authors' intended meaning.

Whenever I began losing the will to live, Toko would rub my knee while Ruriko just kept on doing that big-tit-having thing that she did so well. In this manner we fought our way through Toko's paper and then through Ruriko's; and then they started inviting their pretty friends.

— ¤ —

A few months later, Toko et al visited me to bestow, with great ceremony, some cheap gimcrack they had bought in a tourist trap in Southeast Asia, which provided further motivation for me to make a custom of helping future generations of Asada Girls with their trip prep. I sometimes went so far as to help the token males as well.

The Great Man himself warmed to me and complimented me on numerous occasions, which was uplifting. He was on track to be elected the next dean of International Relations in those days, while I was on track to start a potentially ruinous international relation of my own with an IR sophomore, so there was a nice symmetry to that.

— ¤ —

Eventually, email took over as the preferred means of contact, thus eroding the potential for knee grabbing and cleavage diving. By that time, Asada's dean-ship had come and gone, as had my scandalous liaison. It seemed we had outlived our usefulness to each other. And yet, the man kept on picking intriguing females to whom I was powerless to say no.

Asada Seminar members continued to plague me every minute of every day, none more than notorious sluggard Maki Migita. They left on Sunday, and seemed most grateful.

December 2003

This was the Maki who had destroyed my beautiful wickedness with a plaintive essay during the Christmas Eve make-up class. She still looked all of fourteen even as a junior about to embark on a three-week tour of Asian capitals where girls that age are sold into sexual slavery. I tried not to think about it.

Maki was among the Asada Girls who spotted me in front of the station as I was boarding the bus for my apartment late one November night a few weeks before their departure. They had just finished a post-class visit to a nearby bar, as was clear from the professor's ruddiness and demeanor. The girls, for their part, showed no signs of wear or tear; if there had been unsolicited back-rubbing, they had weathered it well.

"Muggins-san! *Muggins-saaaan!*" came the familiar charismatic bellow, arresting me on the step of the bus. There, as peeved commuters squeezed past me, he explained the evening's activities and spewed effusive, long-winded thanks for all of my assistance lo these many years. His girls, too, he insisted, were grateful. I could make out eight of them in the shadows, as patient and lovely as ever.

Finally, I pried myself loose from his tractor beam and found a seat in the rear of the bus. He could still be heard yammering away out there, and now he had herded his minions into two parallel lines that bowed to me in unison, a spectacle that continued as the bus pulled away, at which point I became aware that at least half of my fellow passengers were staring daggers at the foreigner who had delayed by precious seconds their long trudge home to their families.

Five Disagreeable Things
NU Women Did for Me

The reader presumably knows me well enough by now to understand that I did all the things listed in the previous chapter with a despicable, though unstated, *quid pro quo* mindset.

Alas, the *quo* that I reaped for all that strenuous *quid* was never the hot and buttery sort that I dreamed of. At its most satisfying, the *quo* of NU chicks was apt to manifest itself in the following forms:

1. Shaving my head

On the 24ᵗʰ Mariko Tomuro came to visit with her friends Mio Horii and Asuka Yamamoto. The usual routine: getting my head shaved by beautiful babes, playing my new songs, etc. It was great.

December 1992

This is the earliest reference to the ritual that the archaeological record yields. Context implies that it was not, however, the Ur-shaving.

A bald man has at least a theoretical shot at being sexy; a bald*ing* man, regardless of rebounding skills, does not. That was the lesson I had learned at no charge from Michael Jordan and other NBA icons of the early Nineties.

I bid my barber adieu and bought a shaver. At first I performed the twice-monthly shavings myself until realizing that the increasing stream of female visitors might be harnessed to purpose.

—◻—

That night, sophomore babes Yuri, Naomi and Motoko came over for pizza, songs and head-shaving. In the small confines of my kitchen, where the shaving is done, they mashed their enormous boobs against my head.

December 1993

As the years went by, I recall feeling a certain disgust and shame on those occasions when I failed to lure a willing volunteer to my home before growing shaggy, and had to tend to my own needs. Then, one fine day, one of the full-time English teachers gave me the spare key to the private office that she never used. This was a great boon to head-shaving, as I could now approach NU chicks in their natural habitat rather than waiting for them to come to me.

I was at school every day during the club-recruiting mini-festival last week. On one of those days, freshman guidance was held, but I managed to miss it. I refused to meet the freshmen with a less-than-radiant head, and by the time I found a girl willing to shave me, it was too late.

April 1995

Some responded eagerly enough to the invitation, especially if it could become a memory shared with friends. Others required persuasion and persistence.

Takako Marui, who spurned the chance to do so in April, finally did shave my head.

September 1995

—◻—

Aki Mino was another tough get, despite the fact that she had once famously and on her own initiative sat on my lap in front of a roomful of astonished freshmen while I corrected her study-abroad application essay for her.

Settling her warm, spongy buttocks onto my groin in a manner that might have earned her a hefty tip in a different cultural context wasn't an issue for Aki, but a mere half a hemisphere into the shaving of my head, she squealed *No más!*, or words to that effect. Luckily her asexual companion Daimu was there to step in.

Thanks to my website, on which I routinely posted fetish photos of the act, the notion of shaving the teacher's head became less alien to the NU female population. There were some who came to interpret being asked as an honor, if only in a whitewashing-the-fence sort of way. I have no shortage of photos taken during or just after a shaving with girls cheerfully and proudly clutching or pointing at my head as if it were the carcass of a rhino that they had just bagged on safari.

But that was after the deed was done. Getting started was a whole other matter. Here is what you might have heard had you happened to pass by the door of the private office where two IR girls were taking turns shaving my head. And those office doors at NU were notoriously porous.

[Whirring]

Female 1: Eh? Seriously? We're really doing this?

Male (i.e., me): Yes, seriously! Let's go!

Female 2: Oh... Ahh... Oh, I'm scared!

M: Okay, then, Tatsuko—you go first.

F1: Ohhh... It's so scary... Well, here I go...

[Whirring/buzzing]

M: Ahhh, yessss!

F1 & 2: Wahhhhh-ha-ha-ha-ha-haaaaa!!!

M: It's not working! You have to push harder!

F1: Okay, okay!

M: Harder! *Harder!*

F1: I can't! I can't do it!

M: Here! Grab hold of me here! Yes, yes, like that!

F1: Ahhhhhhh…

M: Now *push!* Push *as hard as you can!* Don't worry, you won't break it.

F1: Ohhhhh!

[Intense whirring/buzzing]

F2: Wow, look at that!

F1: Yes, yes! Oh, it's coming off!

M: Ahhhhhhh…… Oh, that feels *goooooooood…*

F1: Hey, this is fun!

M: Well, share the fun. Let Kana do my other side.

[Whirring, laughter]

At the end of the procedure, the shaver would inevitably ask, "Is that it?" to which I would reply: "Well, I have more hair elsewhere, if you're game" because, you know, I'm so funny.

The plate on the office door bore the name of someone else, making it the perfect crime.

—◻—

After lunch, I had Ichie Kikkawa and Asako Kubo shave my head, making the joy of the day complete. "It's my first time!" Ichie actually squealed—an added service at no extra charge.

November 1995

I never passed up an opportunity to point out to girls just after they had completed the head-shaving process—or sometimes while they were in the midst of it—that, to my mind, the act brought us to a level of intimacy that transcended sex.

The hope, of course, was that some of them would think, *Well, if we've already transcended sex, no harm in going back and filling in the gaps.* The reader can perhaps guess the success rate of this ploy.

Within the head-shaving sphere itself, there were varying levels of intimacy. Group shaving came to be regarded as a chummy but forgettable experience, akin to going out for Chinese. A one-on-one shaving behind closed doors signaled a greater leap of faith for both parties. The ultimate experience was a solo shaving sans shaver, using cream and a razor. Only two young ladies, enshrined forever in my diseased heart, would ever do me that honor.

2. Ostentatiously adoring me in my homemade video

In 1998, with our twenty-fifth high school class reunion looming back in Illinois, my old friend Penniman began to lobby me for some sort of contribution.

"Maybe you could get your hands on a video camera at your school," he suggested. "Just show us what your everyday life is like over there. People want to know."

The project—conceived as a form of revenge porn aimed at girls who wouldn't date me in high school (aka "girls of my high school")—bore the working title "Chicks Who Think I'm Groovy." I set about rounding up volunteers.

Each participant stood alone on a platform at the front of a classroom, coquettishly rocking, fingers knitted behind her back, and recited a paean of her choice from a menu that I had thoughtfully prepared.

Mihoko: Mr. Muggins is soooo groovy. All chicks here in Japan dig him.

Miu: I wanna be his intern.

Anna: He is the man of my dreams!

Chinatsu: I just wanna kiss his shiny head over and over.

Anna again: The sight of him makes me weak with desire! *[Swoons]*

Naomi: It takes a man like Muggins to satisfy a woman like me.

None of those snooty ice princesses from the Mortonville High class of '73 ever had to gnash teeth through the opus, however, as editing the raw footage proved too daunting. Anna, for one, needed several takes before she could nail the swooning to her own satisfaction, and Naomi had an unfortunate tendency to crack up halfway through "It takes a man like Muggins."*

Also, the thing just didn't feel complete without the "money

---

* For those keeping score at home, this was the same tragic Naomi who actually *was* serving as my intern at the time.

shot" that I had conceived. For this, I would have to assemble a veritable multitude of chicks to mill about in the quad. Then I would emerge on the second-floor balcony of Building 5, all ayatollahed out in a turban and flowing black robe, and grimly raise my hands, whereupon they would begin rhythmically throwing their arms in the air while chanting my name, then ululating and writhing spastically. Then I would turn to the camera and intone...

Forty-something women of Mortonville: I condemn you to the dustbin of history!

...Or some similar cold-blooded nonsense cribbed from Ruhollah Khomeini, who really was just the best for that sort of thing.

For all its flaws and its incompleteness, I still break out the raw footage now and then when I need bucking up.

3. Meowing into a microphone over and over and over

Freshman girls Noa Kuramoto, Ikumi Suematsu, Hirona Takahata and Hikaru Hasegawa then came on Sunday the 13th for "Nangaku Woman"... It was the toughest session yet, held on a steamy evening...
September 1996

At the time, I was in the throes of recording my second album—the high-water mark of my obsession with making not just *an* album of stupid novelty songs full of inside jokes in Japanese, but *the* album of stupid novelty songs full of inside jokes in Japanese: an album of stupid novelty songs full of inside jokes in Japanese that would belong to the ages, one that would strangle in the crib any incipient notions in the heads of other songwriters to poach on my genre.

"Nangaku Woman" was intended as something of a Broadway

showstopper. There was a rich horn-heavy arrangement, and the piece built gradually over five minutes to a juddering climax. I sang in the role of an anonymous office worker who spots a group of NU girls on the commuter train one morning, becomes obsessed, and tails them all the way up to the campus, which he finds populated by radiant angels. A sample of the (translated) lyrics:

The scent of them, the way they walk,
Reminds me so much of former prime minister Tomiichi Murayama.
But Murayama, he never trimmed his eyebrows.
Ain't it just like a Nangaku woman
Not to take a back seat to any former prime minister?

Behind this, the female chorus was supposed to throw down…

Nyan nyan nyan nyan nyan nyan nyan nyan…

…the Japanese equivalent of *Meow, meow, meow* (etc.) on a descending chromatic scale. Each also had her own short solo.

I had handpicked Noa for a particular line because of her Japanese-daughter-of-Howard-Cosell intonation, only to discover that her singing voice came out a sweet soprano.

"Sing it the way you usually talk," I said.

"How do I usually talk?"

"Well, you *tawwwk* like *thiiis*," I said, affecting her grating, nasal tone.

"I thought you wanted me because my voice is pretty," she said, clearly wounded.

There ensued a sweaty silence. Then I made them do the whole piece over again. And again, and again, for hours on end, past ten o'clock on a school night, oblivious to their long commutes home, just because I could.

And, you know, art.

4. Tolerating the same two tasteless jokes over and over and over until the last syllable of recorded time

If I ever subjected an NU chick to either of these stunts more than once, it was an accident. But Nanagaku womanhood as a whole had to endure them year after year, for I never tired of either.

Gag One was simplicity itself. On finding a pair of familiar girls staring into, say, the campus bulletin board, I would loom behind them—silently at first, and then begin emitting suspicious groans ("Unnnnhhhh... *unnnnnhhhhh... HUNNNNNHHHHHH!!*") until they warily turned in unison to confront the source. The payoff was seeing their faces cycle through the same series of reactions:

(1) It's a weird guy!
(2) No! It's our teacher!
(3) No! *Both!*

This would invariably be followed by nervous laughter and the not necessarily playful pummeling of my chest with tiny fists.

This bit proved more effective when done off campus, at the local train station or in a convenience store, for example. I assure the reader that I never unleashed the ploy on a lone girl, but always granted them the safety of numbers.

—◻—

September was prime time for Gag Two. I would always return from summer vacation with a bad sunburn on my arms, or even, in years of particular carelessness, on my scalp. Then, during a lull in class, I would approach a seemingly amenable subject, peel off a strip of myself, and publicly offer it to her, because "you might want to clone me someday."

Admonitions to the effect that the item would surely fetch millions of dollars at auction and that the offer would not be repeated failed to quell the vociferous rejection.

5. Letting me live after seeing unauthorized photos on my website

See, this is what happens when a man doesn't have daughters of his own and interacts only with other people's daughters. You just don't get all the little Zen nuggets of wisdom like:

Young ladies might take a powerful dislike to having their picture taken without warning while, say, chomping on a sausage, and then finding that picture on a website frequented by all their classmates.

I had to learn this and many other rules of girl-interaction the hard way, through constant negative reinforcement until it finally sank into my uninsulated, oft-peeling head. As with the housebreaking of a dull puppy, I needed to have my nose rubbed into my mistakes, repeatedly.

For years, I had taken pride in what I called "guerilla photography" because of the macho sheen the name provided, which worked like this:

[FLASH!]

Girl caught gesticulating wildly: Huh?

Girl caught with noodles dangling from mouth: Whahwazzat?

Me: Do you mind if I take your picture?

And wouldn't you know, within a month, the dad-blasted thing would turn up on my website.

I knew that young women as a class tended to be fussy about the publication of their image. Back in the Satan, I had nieces who routinely obsessed over such trifles as a driver's license photo. But I had assumed that NU girls were above and beyond all that. An NU woman with noodles dangling from her mouth was still an NU woman: she still shimmered and inspired awe in a way that mere mortals in their Red Carpet designer gowns could never hope to. Surely they knew that.

Sensing this puppy-dog naivety on my part, NU girl-dom collectively sighed and resolved to let me live. I'm guessing it was one of those five-to-four decisions accompanied by a blistering dissent, though.

—◻—

So that's it. My list of "disagreeable things that NU chicks did for me" ends here, at a paltry five items. Let it be duly noted, however, that the operative words here are "my list." If you could survey the chicks, I suspect that a few addenda would emerge.

"Only You Think
You Are Young"

Youth's a stuff will not endure.

— *Twelfth Night*

First bar party with NU freshmen, one month into my exile from the International Relations Department:

We got stuck at Shirokiya, because the party-master waited too late to reserve Watami or other popular spots. Toshio, the foreign-looking guy whose mother is Israeli, and I stormed the gate first. The girl in charge (who looked about 12) told us that not only we representatives but the whole group would have to show proper IDs before being admitted to drink alcohol. The police were cracking down, she said.

I assured her that these students were my third-year seminar students at Nangaku, and Toshio added that he and I would gladly take responsibility in case of any trouble with the police. We got in. I tried not to think about being raped in prison by Toshio...

Manami Yagi was a doubtful starter because of a cold, but bravely showed up to endure my taunts, my huge color copies of her embarrassing ID picture, and my strange habit of hurling food at her.

I informed Manami that Ryu Sasanuma had recently visited my office, and had taught me the Japanese word nama-iki, *meaning "cheeky, saucy," in reference to her. Manami defended herself from charges of being cheeky by accusing Ryu of being a horny loser despised by all women. She later denounced me for my obvious Peter Pan syndrome. "Only you think you are young," she bellowed, "But you are old!!" I had to admit, that hurt. My parting words to her were, "Fuck you, Manami." Not very original…*

Anyway, it was a fun first party.

May 2003

—◻—

The harsh exchange with Manami occurred as we were leaving the bar, located in a basement, and I challenged one of the boys to race me up a side-by-side pair of down escalators.

The incident sparked a flurry of email between the cheeky and saucy Manami and myself that spanned most of the semester and totaled roughly 8,500 English words. I wrung extra wordage from her by pushing her buttons—"trolling" her, I believe the young folks now call it—at one point extracting twenty-six angry exclamation points from her in a single email, a record that still stands. The extra credit I was able to award her for these English rants allowed me to justify passing her despite her frequent absences from the class, which may have owed to its first-period-in-the-morning slot, or to her loathing of me.

But even if it were the latter, I could take solace in knowing that I would never be her most despised male human, as the aforementioned Ryu Sasanuma served as my buffer in that regard. Any mention of Ryu, who seemed a typically benign sort of NU lad to me, would set her off. "I hate Ryu!" Manami wrote, scarcely pausing to add:

I hate him than any other boy!! I can say 'Fuck you!' to him. He likes girl very much, but most of the girl I know hates him. And he said you that I am cheeky. He has a no right to say that!!! I hate him!! Go to HELL!! Boooooo! He's chicken! Go back to your Mama!!

Did you understand how I hate him?

175

If you did, don't tell me the name "Ryu" never ever!!
That's good thing to you and me…

Oh, last day, I went to Mariah Carey's concert.
My father got the tickets from someone, so I went there.
It was so noisy! I got a head ache after the concert.
But her voice was so beautiful!

In my response, I pointed out that some might say of her, "She's a princess. Go back to your papa!" and reminded her that, in addition to expensive concert tickets, her father was also the source of her expensive ring from Tiffany's—all of which had the desired effect of extracting still more curse-words and exclamation points.

She was a brilliant, hourglass-shaped law major with oddly large teeth who concocted within me a rocket-fuel-like mixture of adoration and exhilaration and fear. At one point I tried to wheedle a promise from her to dance naked on a tabletop at our next class party. She wrote back insisting that I do so instead.

I will take your picture and I can send that to Nangaku Sexual Harassment Center. Then you will be fired!! What a funny thing!!

Neither of us stripped at that inevitable follow-up party, but I did make a point of sitting next to Manami and her lone friend in the class, at one point summoning the courage to tell her why I liked her so much.

"You have very large…*[Manami cringing]* and very beautiful… t…*[now leaning as far away from me as she can without sliding out of our booth]* …t—teeth."

"Stop looking at me," she seethed, as her friend cackled.

She kept sending grippingly furious English messages to me for bonus points until I informed her that grades had already been submitted, after which I never heard from her again.

—◻—

The shift to a new department meant teaching majors of Law, like Manami and her nemesis, Ryu, or Sociology or Business, and thus I could no longer coast on the gamey but generally positive reputation I had built up over a decade in International Relations.

Whenever I had a spirited altercation with an IR girl, I could assume that it rested atop a solid foundation of mutual affection. It occurred to me all too late that my back-and-forth with Manami was built on sand, and it rattled me. She really meant it when she called me old, and she meant it to hurt.

—◻—

It has been a parting-of-the-clouds day in a lot of ways. Morning classes were fun. At lunch I held joint office hours with Yasufumi and hashed over the future of TOEFL classes. Nao Oizumi and Juri Kato dropped by. We flirted with them and recruited them for video work in future curriculum development projects. Nao suggested that they might appear "butt naked." I don't necessarily have to miss the old International Relations vibe after all.

April 2004

My benefactor in the new department, Yasufumi-sensei, wangled me a new contract that took effect that very month. While my NU career still had an expiration date, it had been kicked down the road a few more years. I was getting $25,000 more per annum than I had under my old IR contract, my teaching load had been cut by more than half, and my contract stipulated immunity to stare down the shirts of IR majors between the months of May and October. I made that last part up, but for a giddy moment during the negotiations, it had seemed like I might have had that language worked in.

Nao and Juri were both IR majors, excellent English speakers, and prime shirt-diving material, although a study in contrasts. The former was slim with a tiny heart-shaped face and giant mouth, the latter more of a "straight-to-DVD women's prison movie" gestalt.

177

The four of us passed many a lunchtime office hour together, after which three of us would share equal billing in my nocturnal fantasy.

At the same time, moving away from IR meant dealing with a larger percentage of male students, which required some adjustments.

—◻—

Yuichiro Sakamoto, a Law Department guy in the Tuesday class, has emerged as the most amusing, or most irksome, or both, of my students. He's the only one taking advantage of the "call-my-cellphone" bonus point system, and he desperately needs points. He pops out at me all over town—most recently at the 3-F [convenience store]—just like Kato the houseboy used to attack Peter Sellers. I rearranged a Quiz time just so that he could be in the room when it was given, but he failed it anyway. After that class, he approached me to ask for help in fixing him up with an agreeable middle-aged woman, as he was accustomed to earning money in this manner back in Kita-Kyushu.

May 2004

I still remember the convenience store ambush. He almost seemed to emerge from the walls like one of those liquid-metal Terminators, huge and loud, windmilling his beefy arms around as if to help propel English words from his brain to his mouth.

"I DID NOT GO TO CLASS TODAY! BECAUSE I SLEPT LATE! BUT IT IS OKAY! I WILL CALL YOUR PHONE AND LEAVE AN ENGLISH MESSAGE!"

Yes, yes, that would be fine, I assured him, as all activity in the store ceased.

"IT WILL BE BONUS POINT! I WILL TELL YOU MY FUTURE PLAN! IN ENGLISH! PLEASE EXPECT IT!"

Looking up at him, one could see his Midnight Cowboy appeal to underserved women of a certain age. I actually gave some consideration to pimping him out, as I could think of a few colleagues who might have been mellowed by a little touch of

Yuichiro in the night, but ultimately felt it best to leave him to his own devices.*

—□—

It was warm and humid all week at school and not yet rainy. The cleavage was out in full force and I was running on cleavage power.

June 2004

The [summer "TOEFL Hell" intensive] *class is notable mainly for the abundance of funky, vivacious chicks. I've lost count of how many times I've had to whack off on their account. The tawny and over-exposed Yuka Oh (aptly named, Oh!) alone has inspired four launches at least. I hate to sound disloyal to longtime lust object Nao Oizumi, but it's been the English Department girls that have mainly set me off….*

July 2004

The hot chicks of TOEFL Hell did indeed get a big bump in their scores on the final test of the course, which set off an orgy of celebration on the last day. They took my picture and I, in turn, took theirs, albeit with a different motivation.

It was an absolutely delightful Hell and absolutely exhausting. I honestly intended to show up at school the next day and accomplish some work but ended up flat on my back at home the whole day.

August 2004

---

* One of Yuichiro's even seedier male classmates showed up in the first period still wobbly from a party that had gone on till five. I dealt with the situation by pelting him with dictionaries. It is a long story, so I will leave it at that.

If these vulgar ravings about the beauty quotient in that summer intensive course strike the reader as excessive, know that some nine years later I dug out the photos referenced above as research for this book, and found that the images still retain their magic. It was an almost dangerous concentration of sexiness in one classroom.

Yesterday the blowjob dream team of Rina Asai and Ena Yuge came over to make lunch for me. They stayed five hours. We went through the usual litany of entertainments: pig-throwing, "Hot-or-Not" website, South Park, gossiping about IR people, etc. Moderate to high sexual tension was achieved. I dared to hope for a knock on my door late at night (Ena lives nearby) though I knew the chance was slim.

August 2004

It should be duly noted that, while sexual tension ranged from moderate to high in the space between my ears, it is entirely possible that the rest of the environment failed to register it. There's just no way of knowing what any caring and lovely and lunch-making Japanese chicks are ever thinking about me or any other subject—it is, indeed, that very mystery that inspires me to write books on the topic, hoping against hope that answers will emerge from the process.

—▫—

This entry followed the annual posting of the list of successful applicants for studying abroad. In accordance with tradition, the list was tacked onto a bulletin board in the middle of the campus at noon sharp on a Thursday.

Four of the selectees are unknown to me, but it was, on the whole, a good day for Team Muggins. I had reminded everyone of my existence the night before the selection with my usual "the sun will rise on Friday" email message.

As a result, I got about eight tearful (so it seemed) email responses the next day and one phone call (Nao Oizumi).

I would probably say this any year, but I care more about this bunch than most of the bunches, and it warms my heart that I could help so many worthies to make it over the hump: Rina and Ena and Nao, etc. My only regret is that I could not see them when the news was fresh, to get the usual full-body hugs and feel their heaving titties boring into my sternum. I always like that.*

October 2004

For several of my sweethearts, selection to a study-abroad program was only tentative, conditional on their improving their TOEFL scores still further within a narrow time-frame, so my contact with them only intensified after the selection announcement: incredibly nerve-wracking for them but great news for me.

Nao Oizumi got 213 on TOEFL, leaving Atsushi Ito and Fuyumi as the last stragglers... Fuyumi had another inadequate test today, and I'm not sure what her fate will be. I had prayed for her success today, mainly for her sake but also, to be sure, because it facilitated the fantasy wherein she comes over here and blows me.

April 2005

—□—

In the spring [study-abroad] announcement, Chiaki Kamei and Juri Kato were named the first students to go to New Zealand since Kotoko Inaba went years ago. I wrote to my long-time sexual confidant [Kotoko] to try to get a clear picture on the possibility of getting Chiaki to give me a shirtless handjob in my office.

---

* I know. That had all the earmarks of being the admirable sentiment of a respectable educator and then, *wham*, those last two sentences.

Sorry.

June 2005

Yes, granted, this is all getting to be too much.* I sense the reader grows weary. But indulge me one more:

In the meantime, I was able to squeeze in a jet-lag nap before going off to meet Rina Asai, Ena Yuge and Joji Koyama for dinner at a little bar near the station. After that, it's all an alcoholic haze.

July 2005

Rina and Ena are the very pair I described a few pages back as a "blowjob dream team," a description I still stand by. I had first been drawn toward the sleepy, blinky, tofu-complected Ena, in part because I found Rina more than a bit intimidating.

Rina was tall, lithe, taut, with the BMI of an NFL wide receiver and weapons-grade big brown eyes and a smile that could spread first-degree burns on the epidermises of lonely middle-aged men in seven seconds. She was entirely capable of killing me with just three fingers, tearing my heart out both literally and figuratively in the same instant, and most jocund would I have greeted that end.

---

* But in case you're wondering, here is Kotoko's reply:

About your question; Do Nangaku girls want to do handjob for you thanking you for helping them?

Answer; I'm afraid that few girls think like that because basically we consider you as a "teacher" whom we respect and admire. I guess we look at you somewhat like a "God",leading us to ryugaku [studying abroad]. At least I looked at you like that way. You looked like a God to me!! So, I couldnt think of doing handjob to the God because simply I couldn't imagine clearly that the God has penis!!

I was skeptical. If Nangaku women regarded me as God-like, they had been concealing it well. You don't try to pull God's pants off, or randomly grab His butt-cheek when He walks by your desk, or pluck hairs out of His chest on a whim. But I appreciated the sentiment, anyway. Kotoko was just the best.

In a battle between Rina Asai and Sigourney Weaver's character from the *Alien* series, I would not bet on Ripley. I suppose it would come down to who seized the flame thrower first. Perhaps the reader gets the idea.

When poring over long and unyielding TOEFL passages, Rina would hunch down over the test booklet and spread her legs as widely as a sumo grand champion performing a ring-entering ceremony. The posture was the antithesis of sexy apart from the fact that it broadcast innate confidence and self-possession, traits any thoughtful middle-aged pervert finds alluring in a young woman. *This is the way we concentrate,* her body seemed to say on behalf of her keen mind. *I don't know why we do it this way. We just do.*

On the hot July night in question, Rina, in tight white jeans, led us to a small bar theretofore unknown to me on the far side of the local station. Trailing a few steps behind her allowed me to admire her powerful, feline stride and take photos of her buttocks.

"What are you doing back there?" she asked in response to a flash.

"I am taking photos of your buttocks."

"Why?"

I did not deign to answer.

—¤—

They brought along a boy, Joji, known to me from a regular English class but not remotely a study-abroad candidate. I wondered why he was there. But he was certainly cute enough in his own right, and if they were gearing up for some sort of four-way bisexual marathon, I would endeavor to give satisfaction.

On Friday night at the dinner gathering, they gave me a spanking new jimbei *to wear. After a few gin and tonics (later augmented by the beer and wine), I was back in my old IR party mode, farting out 10,000 yen on the table and then getting my money's worth by snapping photos of Rina's ass. And they also gave me one of those sign boards with their own messages plus those of a few of the others who are soon to depart that reduced my liquored-up self to whimpering tears. All of this made me further resolved to find a way to stay in Nangaku and continue the Lord's work of prepping these people to go abroad.*

July 2005

A message board was not quite my first choice among possible thank-you presents from Ena and Rina, but it sufficed. And I still trot out the buttocks pictures from time to time, and—notwithstanding opinions to the contrary—become convinced that I really am young.

The Last Intern

Who would ever think that so much went on in the soul of a young girl?

– Anne Frank

Dear Muggins,

Hi!;-)

My name is Kuni Bando!
Yesterday, I was so surprised and so happy to find my number on the list.
YES!! I can take your both class! (Monday 5th class and Friday 4th class)

It's unbelievable!
Thank you so much for choosing me*** (^3^)Kiss
Because I wrote such answer
"Because your head is shining!" (Question→Why do you want to take this class?) on your questionaire paper.

Then, I really couldn't think of the answer...
I don't think I can take your class...
In fact, I couldn't answer well on TOEFL test (on Monday 5th class).

Last year, when I was worrying about curriculum, one woman (a senior) told me that "Muggins is so nice teacher! You had better take his class!!!!" (Please give her 10000 point!)

But I had to take another class on the time your class went on, so I couldn't take any of your classes.

It was so pitty...

But!!!! I can see you twice in a week this semester!!

Until your Friday class, I had listend to such reputation, but I hadn't met you directly. I was so happy when I met you on the first time, because you are so fantastic and gentle.

And your head is too dazzling for me to see! I'm really looking forward to your both classes!
*I wanna come to your apartment! * ˆ O ˆ ***
Until such time, I hope your body will not age further...

Please be kind to me ! ! ! ! ! ! ! ! ! ! ! !

International Relations 2ⁿᵈ year, Kuni Bando

— ¤ —

I have had the best April of this decade—one of the best ever. I'm teaching International Relations people again—teaching them meaningful things, making myself useful to others. Kuni Bando, IR sophomore cutie, is winking at me in class and sending me email saying she wants to be my intern.

April 2005

After leaving International Relations in 2003, I spent a year doing far less teaching, which freed me up to spend even more time exchanging suggestive emails with NU chicks and masturbating in my office to their pictures.* Typically, NU responded by promoting me yet again, just as they had done at the outset of my illicit affair with an IR sophomore four years earlier.

They stopped short of offering me tenure—give them credit there. While my contract was extended and enhanced, I still had a sell-by date stamped on my glistening scalp. But in the meantime, life was good.

—◻—

Dear Muggins,

In everyday life, I lack for nothing, so I go to university, have a chat with friends, do club activity, sometimes go to dinner party with friends, and go to bed easily.
There is no need to think about difficult things.
But there are plenty of time to read newspaper, to watch TV news, to read academic magazines.
When I prepare for TOEFL, I need not only develop English skill, but also acquire education.

See! there is also my earnest side.
Friends often say "You are the optimist! You're always thinking sweets and making people laugh!"...

Thank you for reading!
See you!

Kuni

—◻—

If Kuni were heaven-sent, she was not of that quadrant of Heaven

---

* For some odd reason, I was given a shared office that year, but was never assigned a roommate. Which was advantageous, as the masturbating might have proven awkward.

that churns out the limber, top-heavy Victoria's Secret angels that were NU's stock in trade. Kuni was from old-school Heaven, home base of Cupids and other childlike cherubs, creatures so presexual as to seem androgynous when they weren't caught peeing into fountains.

She was roughly the size and shape of one of your lankier koalas, with a broad pumpkinish head. Her tiny mouth sat slightly askew on her face, always poised to spew a derisive titter as she lay in wait for any miscue or blunder on my part, as, for example, when she barged into my office without knocking late one afternoon and caught me asleep at my desk.

I tried to deny it, only to be betrayed by the string of saliva connecting my chin to the pool that had formed on the desktop. She quickly set about reporting this to her vast network of friends. In retrospect, I can take solace in the fact that there was no Twitter yet.

—◻—

The following came in response to a relatively perfunctory email in which I expressed generic satisfaction with her latest in-class TOEFL essay.

Dear Muggins,

Thank you so much, my wanderful teacher...
I had read half of your mail, I cried because your words made so.

Was my essay the longest?
Oh, it's surprising!
But It's my habitual thing to write longer.
I do like writing something, as you know, I write Email everday, these days, so
I rarely be in trouble to write long sentences.
But when I write essay, that is not so much pursuasion.

I write essay as I conceive. [Editor's clarification: "I just type anything that pops into my pumpkinesque head."]
So I noticed that I have to make outline at the beginning!
Anyway, your praising made me happy very much!!! Thank you!

>if you want to apply for studying abroad this year, I'm sure you could be a strong candidate, and I will support you.

This sentence also made me cry...
Because it's so delightful!

Probably today, we'll have the explanation about "one year study-abroad".
I'll have the club training after 3rd period, but I skip it and go to your explanation meeting.
In my club, the girls are so nice and cute, maybe you'll fall in love with some of them, but the boys are.......n..ice...
NO!!!
Telling a lie is not good thing!
My parents often say so!
To tell the truth, some boys look like oyaji [middle-aged men—Ed.]
One or two seniors are nice, (but those nice seniors have already snatched up the cute freshman girls! How fast they work! Those girls have only been in the club for a month!) but others...are a little strange...

Keep smiling!
Good bye!

your cute assistant
Kuni

My reply:

Well, you're not the first Nangaku girl that I made cry. I have a feeling that one day you're going to make me cry, too...

Anyway, everything I wrote was true.

Well, I'm sorry that you can't be satisfied with boys in the hiking club.

> *To tell the truth, some boys look like oyaji.*

What's wrong with that? Do you discriminate against middle-aged men?

> *One or two seniors are nice, (but those nice seniors have already snatched up the cute freshman girls! How fast they work! Those girls have only been in the club for a month!)*

It is the natural way of the world. I think the most miserable creatures on earth are freshman boys (not only in Nangaku, but in any university in the world). They are surrounded by beautiful freshman girls. But they watch, helplessly, while older boys take away their dream girls one by one... They can only watch, and cry...

But one day, they will be the older boys who take away freshman girls. Such is the way of the world. It is as natural as lions eating zebras.

Muggins

Your ideas about the love between seniors and freshman girls and boys are really interesting!
You have a special watching eyes to research love affair.
Your interesting songs also tell us that.
"Such is the way of the world. It is as natural as lions eating zebras."
It's maxim!

I'm not really busy so I can write Email to you,

But I do know you are so busy and you are popular among girls even if boys?!!?
you may have to write Email to them or have a party with them.
so, I don't care if your reply is late.
Or even you can't give me a mail.
I hope that you have a good sleep and be in blood!!!!

Needless to say, I'm really happy to take mail from you!

Kuni

—◻—

A month into the 2005 school year, as I sat down to update my journal, I broke open a fine whine...

I wonder how seriously Kuni is flirting with me, and what I will do about it. I honestly wonder <u>what I will do about it</u>.

...then realized in mid-paragraph that, at forty-nine years of age, the question of what to do about a perky nineteen-year-old genius who winks at you and clamors to be your intern was not exactly a worst-case scenario, grappling-with-midlife-dilemmas-wise.

Among my high school classmates back in Mortonville, there were those coping with downsizing, of both the corporate and erectile types—not to mention debilitating illnesses—while my most pressing concern was reining in the relentless ninety-five-pound pumpkin-headed sophomore who would serve as my intern throughout my final two years at Nangaku.

Her duties consisted of checking the Japanese content I wrote for my self-aggrandizing website, offering feedback on my original class materials, and helping me prepare applications to other universities. She was prompt and superb at all these tasks. I paid her out of my research budget.

As a former president could have told you in that year of 2005, one never really knows where these intern-supervisor relationships are going to take one. Interns are like a box of chocolates, I seem to recall some philosopher musing. Some will leave you craving more while others plunge you into diabetic shock.

— ⌑ —

More exchanges from the email archives:

And here is one more thing that I want to tell you!
Your jokes are really good! I'm serious! It's true!
I wonder why they don't laugh so much in that class.
In Japan, we are taught that we shold be quiet and polite in calsses (too much).
But I think there is no need to be always quiet.
I think sometimes..... NO! MANY times, Japanese customs and manners are not good.
Go back to main issue.....
Please have a confidence in your jokes!!
Your jokes really make me happy!
(these days, somehow I'm sour, I feel...I don't know why...so your jokes were really good for me!!!!Thank you, Muggins!)

Sincerely,
KUNI

Kuni,
    In order to make you officially my intern, I have to tell the General Affairs people your home address. Can you send it to me (in Japanese)?
    I promise I won't become your stalker.

Muggins

Muggins,
It's okay to be my stalker! >_ • (wink)

[Address redacted – Ed.]

Kuni

That's kind of you, but stalking is too hard! Young girls move around too much. I get tired easily. I just want to lie down and rest... I'm too old to stalk... (Sigh...)

Also, I'm afraid of your father. *[A high school principal – Ed.]* If he catches me stalking you, maybe I'll have to stay after school and clean the teachers' room.

Muggins

—▢—

Dear Intern,

Thanks for returning one part of the work. I was able to update my home page a little with a new song, thanks to your efforts.

As for the test on Monday, I have no comment. I have not checked the essay-AAAAAAAHHHHHHHHHH!!!!

Sorry. I was just watching "Hodo Station," and Furutachi is wearing the ugliest jacket I've ever seen. He looks like a very unhappy clown...

As I was saying, I haven't checked your essay yet so I can't know your total score. Maybe tomorrow I'll know it, but I won't tell you...

How about that other job? When you finish it, I will take you out to dinner anywhere in Yokohama that you want to go.

Benevolent Despot

Muggins,

I finished the big work somehow or other.
Please check it and use abusive language against me....
I will check it over again and again as far as possible.
I'll cooperate your HP renewal project!

P.S.
It took 3hours and a half to finish this task.

I hope you don't take a dislike to me....
;_;

Love, Kuni

Hello, my dear intern

Thank you for returning the tape, and for the nice snack.

Is it true that you will be someone else's intern this summer? It's like uwaki *[an illicit affair – Ed.]*... But I forgive you because uwaki is one of my hobbies.

Did you choose the restaurant that you want to go to for your reward? I can go any night next week except Friday and Saturday. After that, the next chance is the weekend of August 5-6.

Of course you can get money for your work, too. We should meet at school some day next week to do the paperwork. What day will you come?

Your tired supervisor,
Muggins

Welcome back!!!!!
I've been wainting for you for a long time!

This week, I'll go to Nangaku on Monday, Wednesday and Thursday!

And here is one suggestion.
I want to invite Chiyo and Yudai to the dinner.
Chiyo always helps me and teaches lots of English, and Yudai loves Muggins and often says that he wants to talk with you. Maybe he is jealous of me?
Is it OK?

I'll go to your office anytime you assign.

Kuni

Ha! I knew it! You're afraid to be alone with me, aren't you?
    Well, you are a clever girl...
    Yes, I suppose it's okay if those two come along. Still, it's *your* reward dinner. You should choose a restaurant and I will pay half the bill. The others must pay for themselves.

Muggins

YesYesYes!!!!
Because I know that one of your hobbies is uwaki.
I'm afraid of your sexy seducing...

I'll tell them your suggestion about the account.
Thank your for your proposition!

And, here is one idea.
The party day, August 5th is the Yudai's birthday!
Chiyo told Yudai that August 5th meeting is the party that only Yudai and Chiyo join.
Yudai doesn't know that Muggins and I will go to the dinner.
Yes!
It's SURPRISE (HAPPY BIRTHDAY, YUDAI) PARTY!!!!!!!!
Muggins will celebrate his birthday, Yudai will be surprised and happy more and more.

P.S.
Please keep it secert!
Don't tell Yudai about that during TOEFL CLASS!!

Kuni

—◻—

Even by the standards of my relationships with age-inappropriate NU girls, this was an odd duck of a romance. She never visited my home, not even with friends. I don't remember even speaking to her on the phone.

While not entirely absent from my fantasy rotation (as Kotoko, that other indefatigable correspondent, was), she was likely to be elbowed aside during foreplay by comelier peers named Manatsu and Mirai and Shion before the gears started meshing.

Apart from a very lengthy email correspondence, the relationship unfolded as a series of unannounced visits to my office, where she would burst in without knocking in a state of agitation, like a miniature Japanese Kramer.

She would then sit very close to me, grab me in one of my

extremities (though never the one that clamored for grabbing), and prattle to me about the latest doings at NISH, the dormitory for the University of California students, bandying about names like Christian and Jared and Bradley as if they were celebrities who were supposed to matter to me. My failure to sustain interest in these poorly drawn characters never failed to dismay her.

I'm sure the UC boys liked her well enough, but not in the way that she wanted to be liked. I came to feel that she was, vis-à-vis the UC boys, something comparable to a Fag Hag, and sometimes considered explaining this analogy to her before realizing that it would be too long a walk, at the end of which she would feel wounded.

Typically, our face-time interactions would follow the pattern of so many of our email exchanges: They would begin on a business tone—

Me: *How many hours did you spend on this transcription?*

Or, Her: *What are you trying to say in this paragraph of your cover letter?*

—before devolving into personal matters, most frequently her lack of a boyfriend or any likely prospects for corralling one. Then there would be whining and pity-partying and the shaking of her remarkably pumpkin-like head until I would say, "Oh, for the love of God, I'll deflower you myself!" Had the offer ever been accepted, I was resolved to follow through on it; but the offer was never accepted.

In any event, whatever sexual tension might have been generated during those frank exchanges in my office would dissipate as soon as I pulled one of my patented, unintentional *oyaji* moves, like mopping the top of my sweaty head with a handkerchief. That was considered hilarious. The way that I blew my nose was another surefire killer.

In short, daily life in 2005 became entirely Kuni-centric, though Fantasy Hour remained crowd-sourced.

— ◻ —

Sunshine is too dazzling to me, the fireworks are too beutiful to me....
Every train I ride on is full of happy couples.......
This summer is the last time that I'm teenager.......
I feel lonely every day.....

BUT!!!!!!!
Tomorrow, I'll go to beach with new,nice swimwear, and with my pretty friends to meet nice guy!!!!! hahahahahaha!!!!!!
I'll report it later!!!!

Crazy girl KUNI

I don't believe you are going to the beach tomorrow at all. I think it's a lie. If you want to prove it's true, you have to bring me pictures of you in nice swimwear.

Thank you.

Anyway, I have more important things to worry about. About 10 minutes after the start of the first day of TOEFL Hell, I totally fell in love with Manatsu Mori, your classmate. I realized that I want to spend the rest of my life with Manatsu Mori. But just as I began to think so, she sat next to YUDAI!!

By the way, Yudai got the highest score on the first test. But on today's test, a freshman girl from Sociology defeated him. Ha!

Jealous Muggins

You can't see the picture of me in nice swim wear, because I'll be naked* in the beach.
If you glance at the picture, you'll be covered with nosebleed.

You are reallllllllly good at uwaki.
Manatsu is one of my English class mates.
It goes without saying* that Manatsu is beautiful and popular,but she lost the popularity any more.....
She was the idol in our class, and many guys were knocked out* by her.

Confidentially......... Yudai is also one of the guys knocked out* by Manatsu.
And sadly, he was knocked out* in the literal sense*......poor Yudai.....
We cheered Yudai up* through the last year...
Her beuty is a severe crime....

>By the way, Yudai got the highest score on the first test.

I saw it yesterday! Say in other words, Yudai showed off* the score paper!

I hope you can get a real love with evil Manatsu!!!!!!

Kuni in the sea

(* Signifies expression from the vocabulary list for our class that she is trying out.)

How was your boy-hunting (fishing?) at the ocean? Did your naked swimsuit work well?

I met many nice guys at the ocean today!!!
My "naked" plan seemed to go well.

See you tomorrow!!
I'm really looking forward to meet you and have a party!
Let's have a nice dinner tomorrow♪♪
naked KUNI in the living

— ¤ —

There's no doubt about it now: my intern is in heat. She embarked on a deliberate boy-hunting trip to the beach. She told me that she went there naked. She uses the word naked *a lot…*

On Friday night I treated her to dinner at a restaurant in Marui, as I had long promised to. The event morphed into a surprise birthday party for Yudai. Chiyo Noda also came. It was a pretty typical International Relations affair. They (mainly Chiyo) bitched about IR English classes…a lot. Todd Plotz seems to be chasing that horrible woman from ten years ago for the title of Most Despised English Teacher of All Time… In fact, Todd may already have the title sewn up… Kuni was offended that he had asked her out. (Sort of an ironic thing to complain about to me, but there it was…) All of them praised me mightily, saying that I had the full package of teaching skill and humanism. Even the Vulcan-like Yudai was effusive. It was very heartwarming.

Kuni showed me phone pictures that were taken on the beach. She wasn't naked, but her bikini was small. One shot was a close-up she had taken of her own lower body. Later, while telling of a girl at the beach who had a tattoo high up on her thigh, she hiked up her skirt to show me the corresponding location.

August 2005

Once you got over the oblong shape of her head—and once you had become a pathetic, poorly socialized, essentially friendless and oversexed forty-nine-year-old heterosexual white man—you had to admit that there was something quite fetching about this intern. A day without a dash of Kuni was…well, not quite a day.

— ¤ —

Muggins

First of all, today,we're sorry for being late.
and thank you for coming to our crazy(←only me)party!!!!!
Maybe Chiyo felt refreshed for your listening to her talking about evil Todd.

I was also very happy to have a nice party and talk with you more than usual campus life.
I realized it again that you are really attractive person!!!!

We are thinking about holding your birthday party for real!!!
Next time, we'll make you more drunken and talk more about your funny stories.

Tomorrow, I have to go to TOKYO campus for club activity.......
It's troublesome.
We'll have 3or4 km jogging festival!
Yeah!!!..............haaaaaa-----(sigh)

Good night!

*humpty dumpty KUNI in the living**

I got over being upset about your lateness, so don't worry about it. I was glad to be invited out, as I seldom go out these days.

Yudai looked surprised? Do you think so? I think he just had his usual blank face. I wish I could be so inscrutable like Yudai... Then maybe I would be surrounded by hot chicks all the time, like Yudai in TOEFL class...

* I never did crack this "in the living" bit; when you're bantering with Japanese chicks and you claim the Home Language Advantage, sometimes you just have to roll with this sort of thing.

Oh, by the way, thank you for showing me various parts of your body. It was more interesting than I had expected. I am hoping to see more of you...

Evil Muggins

—¤—

Perhaps it is time to describe some of the planetoids and other detritus spinning around the Kuni-verse, including one gas giant.

Lesser entity	Was Kuni's...	Ruthless physical assessment	Presents as...	Played by...*
Chiyo	Sidekick	Short-order cook too fond of own wares	Perfectly bilingual due to childhood in the Satan; irony-enabled.	Janeane Garofalo
Yudai	Unacknow-ledged love and lust object	Boy-band skinny, or lab assistant skinny depending on one's viewpoint	Well-groomed, brilliant and unflappable. He even had the straight, diacritical, seemingly penciled-in eyebrows of a Vulcan. A no-brainer for the study-abroad selection.	John Cho
Manatsu	Hot frenemy	Japan Airlines flight attendant	Kuni would never admit to despising her, though I soon discovered that any favor-able mention of Manatsu was sure to resuscitate Kuni's flirtations toward me whenever they began to flag. So Manatsu became that rare beauty who served a useful purpose beyond mere masturbation fodder.	Katherine Heigl.
Todd Plotz	Teacher of sophomore English	Stay Puft Marshmallow Man	An avowed Maoist, Todd would turn any subject into a class warfare lesson, and woe to those who resisted indoctrination.†	Wayne Knight

* I'm going with actors who were marketable in the same mid-2000s time frame. Renée Zellwegger stars as Kuni.

† That spring, on an essay test to select applicants for a short-term summer program in the Satan, I posed the question "What steps should be taken to improve English education at Nangaku?" eliciting from one of Kuni's classmates a screed that could have been titled "Let's Kill and Gut Todd Plotz." The girl managed to milk over 300 handwritten words out of this thesis in only thirty minutes, and you could feel the capitalist oppression she was inflicting on her poor, exploited pencil with every tortured letter.

—◻—

Some works in the Ministry of Finance intern [her summer job – Ed.] *are boring, but others are intersting.*
Other intern student from other universities are very efficient and kind to me.
Our boss is very gentle and charming man.
There are so many good taste(?) men in Marunouchi. [Tokyo's Wall Street – Ed.]
They look like sophisticated and cultivated.
So......Going Tokyo everyday is little hard work for me, but some nice men heal me.

I'm looking forward a lot of works from you!

Kuni

I used to work in Marunouchi. I remember that every man looked like a model in a Konaka Suits commercial. Except, they were all smoking. (In those days it was okay to smoke anywhere in Marunouchi.)
 I haven't prepared your job yet. I will work on it next week.

Me

PS: I got an erotic email from Manatsu Mori.

Show me the erotic Email from Manatsu!!!
My dear teacher is far away.........

I attached some photographs in the Ministry of Finance!!

205

There are some intern friends in the photo.
*Check it out^__^*

I'll leave for Aichi tonight by midnight bus ! (with my friend...not Marunouchi guy....)
I'm really looking forward to go to Aichi-Banpaku!! [aka "Expo 2005" held in Aichi Prefecture that summer – Ed.]
Have you gone to Banpaku?

Well, my message from Manatsu is deeply private so I won't show it to you. But I will summarize the contents.

First, she told me about her recent score on a real TOEFL test. And then... Well, that was it. It was very short. Actually, she didn't write any erotic things, but when I saw the name "Manatsu Mori," I felt very excited and erotic.

Thank you for your pictures. It's nice to have a picture of you wearing clothes for a change.

I have never been to Banpaku. Did you ride the gondola and make an Adult Video?*

Me

—◻—

Intern,

Here is a job for you. I apply for a job in D University. They want a teacher who can use Japanese well. Therefore I should send them both the English and Japanese versions of my CV. Please check the content of my Japanese CV. Notice that I erased

---

* A film crew had been arrested doing so at this Banpaku some weeks before.

the years so that you can't figure out how old I am. Ha-ha-ha.

This is not so urgent, but if you could possibly do it before next Monday it would help me a lot. As always, keep a record of the amount of time that you spend.

Me

Why do you want to hide your age so much.
In places, many "19??" make me burst into laugh.

I don't want to do this job!!!
Because this means that you will go far away,isn't it?
I hope you pass the DU selection, but I feel sad if you would quit NANGAKU teacher...

However,ahem, I'm not a spoily child, so I'll do my best for your bright future!!
I promise that I'll finish this job by tonight or tomorrow night.

I registered as buddy [for University of California foreign students].
I've been really lokking forward to meeting them!!!
Their Japanese skill are very very nice! I was surprised! Many students can greet in Japanese, and moreover, some students can write Hiragana, Katakana, and even Kanji!!!!!!!!!!
I was knocked out.......

*This afternoon...I'll have a *date*!!But I don't know who he is. It's funny, isn't it? It's very mysterious...I'll talk about this later.*

Have a nice weekend!

Kuni

—◻—

Kuni has a blind date with some guy tomorrow...

September 2005

—◻—

If it makes you feel better, my application for another job probably won't succeed. When such an excellent job opening appears like DU, about 300 gaijins will apply for only 1 position. That's not an exaggeration. 300 applicants is common.[*]

You will say, "But you are the best teacher!" (I know because we have a telepathy connection.) Perhaps it's true that I'm the best teacher, but the university really doesn't care about hiring an excellent teacher. Rather, they want someone who has a great career of research. My research is very small and poor.

Do you feel better now?

Hmm... I don't know which topic makes me feel more jealous: you being a buddy, or you having a blind date. I don't worry about the blind date so much. Usually such a person is very ugly. He was ugly, wasn't he? Or egoistic or stupid. Surely something is wrong with him.

Being close to UC students all the time puts your chastity in great danger. I fear it... Be careful.

Me

>You will say, "But you are the best teacher!" (I know because we have a telepathy connection.)

---

[*] "300" was, in fact, an exaggeration. Even so, this application was Quixotic.

Ahem, today, it looks that radio wave of telepathy is in bad condition......
I don't remember saying that "You are the best teacher!!".....
My best teacher is....

> My research is very small and poor.

Please don't say such a thing. when it comes to think of it, in both Muggins class I take, all documents is your hand-made!!!

IR English teachers use not so attractive texts in classes. Your papers are warm and interesting!!

>Usually such a person is very ugly. He was ugly, wasn't he? Or egoistic or stupid. Surely something is wrong with him.

Why you know it?????? Yes, I can't help admitting it...He was not so cool...Moreover, he was too big for me.

I'm 152cm. He is about 190 cm. We hardly see each other's eyes. I saw only his chest...

Kuni

He is 38 cm taller than you. Well, think about this: It's better than dating a man who is 38 cm shorter than you.

Anyway, thanks again for your hard work. I will probably send you some small things for my website soon. But TOEFL Hell will start tomorrow, so I'll become busy.

Me

My last summer in teenager is close to end..........
I'm soooooooo sad....

I forgot this important information!
Next week, we'll go to Okinawa for 4 days.
So I can't use this computer and can't see Email.

Of course Yudai is one of the members.
And you know all the member in the group.
We're thinking about going to traces of war, because 60 years has passed since the war ended. But of course we'll go to the beautiful beach.....white sand, blue sky and water.....
I'll buy some nice food or drink to you!!

My grandparents often say "Busy is only thing that you can feel in the young generation!!"

Kuni

Your trip to Okinawa sounds like fun, but I have a suggestion. Why don't you invite Manatsu Mori to Okinawa? And then take a lot of pictures of her on the beach in her swimsuit, and then give them to me?

Just a suggestion.

Me

Okinawa suggestion is really nice!!
Maybe Yudai will be happy.
And I don't know what is he going to do on the beautiful beach with

Manatsu...
It's too awful to imagine..

Kuni

—¤—

Dear Muggins,

I came back!!and also bronzed Yudai came back!!
We had a very important and fruitful experiences in Okinawa.
I want to talk to you about this trip later.

Dude, you totally slept with Yudai, didn't you? It's okay. I don't mind... Well, not much...

Anyway, tell me about it later.

Me

—¤—

Whereas the DU application had been the longest of shots, my next try, with RU, was fraught with the peril of an actual, bona fide tenure-track offer. I was already doing a day of classes as a part-timer at RU, where some regular faculty members had been hearing my praises sung for years by their NU friends. If they were also hearing about the gamier side of my NU career, they were not letting it dissuade them.

For my part, I found about as much allure in a tenure-track position at RU as I did in Vice President Cheney's taint, but I was down to the last two years of my NU contract, and well past the age at which most institutions would consider me even for shutcho host duties. More significantly, I had quietly released my first memoir—the one meticulously outlining my long affair with an NU sophomore—as a self-published paperback that spring. And sales were starting to pick up.

Thus, it was not so much a door that was closing on my career as a vise. And I was completely dependent on Kuni's assistance to get me out of it by helping me prepare application materials.

—◻—

You are hastening to complete these papers, and they are very important materials, right?
I can't find any excuse words..........

Here is one information.
I came back to my home from the first day in Fall semester with.......
BRONZED YUDAI!!!!!!!
He said, "I'm looking forward to meeting Manatsu and Shion in tomorrow's English class. hahaha!!!!!!"

Kuni

—◻—

I feel very close to the 2004 entering class, to Kuni and ... Yudai and all their vast network of friends and acquaintances. I had not anticipated getting this caught up emotionally in my people at this age and at this stage in my Nangaku career (with one foot out the door). I sort of figured I'd be getting so remote from students due to age anyway that it wouldn't make much difference whether I was at Nangaku or RU or wherever. But instead, the uniqueness of Nangaku students, IR ones in particular, is asserting itself like never before.
Sometimes I feel like punting the RU interview on purpose...

October 2005

—◻—

Dear slimy teacher,

"Splash!" was very intersting! I liked it!
Mirai, sitting next to me was very surprised how young Tom Hanks was.
On the other hand, I was surprised how beautiful Mirai was. Her beauty is heightening day by day.
I heard that Mirai thought Yudai and me were lovers!! I laughed heartily. But she looked serious...
We talked about your class. Of course, both of us think Monday & Friday class are both good.
Moreover, we talk about how intelligent you are!!
We rarely feel tired in class, and we forget time flowing.
I think your time participation is great. [Perhaps "time management" – Ed]
Some teachers often end classes more earlier or later than regular time.

I'm really looking forward to watching the movie in next week!

My beautiful pictures in Okinawa are not arranged yet, but I'll show them as soon as possible!

Kuni

[Editor's note: Mirai, an English major, was a leading contender for one of the UC spots in that fall's study-abroad selection. She had long, silky hair and a cool type of beauty that could freeze-dry fireflies in mid-flight.]

Dear Intern,

Thanks so much for organizing a wonderful celebration of my birthday. I was happy to be remembered, and to have everyone sing a song, and to get cake, and other things.

I regret that I did not finish the lesson earlier so that we could have a party in class. I did not know that you had that kind of a plan. You seemed a little upset after that. If it's because you couldn't carry out your plan completely, well, it's too bad, but I was still very happy. Or if you thought that I didn't appreciate your effort enough, then I'm very sorry. I really, really appreciated it.

The best present I got during this year has been your existence. No kidding.

I will think about you while I selfishly eat all of the cake by myself...

Me

—◻—

I think I hurt Kuni's feelings by not backing her up and trying to get everyone to stay for snacks and chat. She put forth so much enthusiasm, as per her usual idiom. She obviously adores me and I did not return the favor adequately. She was in tears for a while, being consoled by Chiyo Noda. I don't know the upshot of that yet. After I came home and ate half my cake, I emailed her to smooth things over but have yet to receive a reply.

   ...

Kuni emailed me, pooh-poohing the notion that she would cry for so trivial a reason as my birthday party. It was a UC boy who broke her heart. Goddamn it.

October 2005

—◻—

Yesterday, while Yudai, Mirai, etc., were having their big interview *[for the study-abroad selection – Ed.]*, I was also having an interview at J University. Of course they did not offer me a job immediately. I will wait about a week for a decision. The salary looks very good, and many things about this position are superior to Nangaku—especially long vacations with no meetings or duties. I hope they reject me, because otherwise it will be a difficult decision for me...

Me

Good morning!

J University.....It is located near to my granparents house.

Which do you choose good salary or.....us?
There are two more years of our campus days in NANGAKU.

See you later!
Kuni

Sorry if I was rude today. Of course I would have been delighted to have dinner with Mirai (oh, and you and Yudai, too), but I'm not the kind of impulsive person who changes his plans so suddenly, and I had already spent over 500 yen for dinner stuff. Sometime, if you make a plan in advance, I will be happy to join.

Tonight I updated my website a little and I removed the page which contains Manatsu's and others' pictures. I don't understand the objection... Can't an English teacher put no-permission pictures of his pretty students on the internet? Why not???... Sometimes I hate the 21st century...

Well, I'm haunted by your recent question about my position with J University...

> *Which do you choose good salary or.....us?*
> *There are two more years of our campus days in NANGAKU.*

I also have two more years at Nangaku. That is the maximum length of my contract. At the end of that time, Nangaku will throw me away like an old towel.

If I could fly to heaven on the wings of angels in March 2008, that would be perfect. Unfortunately, I think I will probably spend another 30 years on the earth, and so I have to make a plan for that.

Furthermore, I suspect that you will get tired of me even before you graduate.

Me

You were not so rude. Who was rude is me.
If I were you, I would have made the same decision. Because I'm not the kind of impulsive person too.

Manatsu were not so serious, I think, but she was maybe just surprised.
Don't worry about that.
21st century give us lots of liberty though,I don't feel so.

Please note I'm not a "usual" IR student.
I don't intend to make you confused!

I'll tell you ASAP when we have a party!

Goodnight!

Well, I went to Tokyo campus yesterday to meet with all the professors of the English Department. As I told your class last week, they are ugly. Nice guys, but really painful to look at. I really wished I could be looking at Mirai and Shion and Mei (of JC department) and Runa and Genius Girl Arisa and Chiyo and you and many others. But I can't see any of you for at least 10 more days... Sigh...

Disgusted Muggins

Yesterday, you failed to turn on the light over and over.
It was because the beautiful hip appeared in the movie...?
You looked really upset.ha-ha.
Come to think of it,on the return road yesterday, Yudai looked very happy than usual....

Have a nice weekend with her beautiful hip!

P.S.
Yesterday, I went to NISH to have a birthday party of my byddy girl, Alicia.
I had a really nice time with UC students.
And........ Christian gave me a bottle of wine....
I'm still too young to drink "CIANTY"....

Sincerely,
Kuni with UC guy

[Editor's note: We had watched the scene from *Splash!* in which Darryl Hannah, shot from behind, emerges nude from the ocean at the Statue of Liberty. After stopping the tape, I struggled to identify the correct switch to turn the room lights back on. This is a classic example of how petty blunders on my part could set my intern off.

The latter reference to "hip" seems to indicate an assumption on her part that I will re-watch the Darryl Hannah scene in the privacy of my home on a continuous loop all weekend, because her mind cannot yet fathom the far greater wonders available on the internet in the Year of Our Lord 2005.]

—◻—

Certainly, the "butt scene" of Splash is nice, but I thought the previous scene (underwater swimming) was more erotic and revealing.

But Yudai likes butts? Well, *junin toiro* [*"To each his own"—Ed.*]

> *Sincerely,*
> *Kuni with UC guy*

I think the only reason you sent this message was in order to tell me that you are with a UC guy. You think I'll get jealous, don't you? Ha!

I say, "Ha! Ha!"

Ha!
Me

One guy who is 36 is now fallin' love with Manatsu.
No, it's one-sided love.
From "36 guy"...? From Manatsu...?
I can't tell you.....

See you on the 5th period!

Is he a UC guy? In any case, I'm all for it. You might think that I would be jealous and try to protect Manatsu. But above all, I am a supporter of the "Oyaji Team." Whenever any member of our team has a big success, we should all cheer for him. Go, UC Oyaji! Fight, fight!

Me

Now, I'm thinking about one important thing.
It's not about Christian, not about Yudai, not about Mugg...NO!NONO!
But it relates to my future.

IT'S NOW OR NEVER.
I'm thinking...But one of my friend always says to me "You're thinking toooo much."
It's time to decide.

The closer 19th Chirstmas day ... and my 20th B.D. will be, the longer time I'm lonely will be......... [Translation: "Soon I'll celebrate Christmas as a nineteen-year-old and immediately afterward mark my twentieth birthday—both, most likely, without a companion, which makes me feel that much lonelier." – Ed.]

OYAJI is immortal!
Kuni

I see.

Before they become adults, boys all want to have sex. Girls want to have a companion.

Having sex is relatively easy. In the worst case, one can just find a person who will do it for money (or ask an English teacher). But companionship is harder to find.

"Don't think about it too much" is actually good advice. When I was young, I always had better success with girls when I wasn't trying.

I forgot the rate per hour that we agreed for your payment. Anyway, how does 8000 yen for all your work sound? I have to pay you soon, after all. The office wants to finish all payments for this year soon.

Me

Muggins, my early Santa Cruise,
Enough is enough!←Does it make sense?
I'm content with that, thank you very much.

Kuni

The TOEFL practice test on Saturday with Manatsu, Mirai, etc., began from 1:00. I was in my office eating a [box lunch] very quickly before the class. I dropped a small wiener sausage on my lap. It made a big red stain on the crotch of my white pants.

I was embarrassed. I couldn't let Manatsu see me with a big red stain, so I rubbed a wet tissue on my pants. This action successfully got rid of the red stain, but then the crotch of my pants had a big wet spot. I hoped that my pants would dry before 1:00, but they were slow to dry. Therefore, I went to see Manatsu with a big wet spot on the crotch of my pants.

It was not a good day...

Me

—◻—

I just spent a whole Saturday looking at Kazane Orimo, Manatsu Mori, and Mirai Yamada. I think my middle-aged brain is going to blow up...

Me

Muggins,

Monday except you was not good.......I felt sad!

[Editor's note: I think she was aiming for "Monday *without* you," as I had to cancel classes to attend an all-day faculty gathering at the Tokyo campus.]

    I missed you yesterday, too. Professors are not bad people, but they are ugly. Soooo ugly. Like creatures on the bottom of the ocean...

Yoroshiku,
Me

English has many pregnant expressions. sometimes I'm surprised and admired.

Bad version Kuni in my house

—◻—

Kuni dropped by [the office]*on Wednesday noon with Manatsu Mori in tow just so that I could cheer up by looking at Manatsu. Manatsu evidently was fine with this. This is the sort of thing I'll miss about Nangaku. At the same time, Kuni made me sad by poking me in the gut and telling me I'm pudgy. This after 31 days of no alcohol.*

December 2005

—◻—

In mid-December, my contact within RU informed me that the Faculty of Letters there had decided to postpone the hiring of a new non-Japanese professor one year. I was encouraged to reapply the following year. But for the nonce, like the merchant of Venice, my ships had all miscarried; I would spend another year at NU, at the mercy of my intern and her pretty friends.

I told her as much to her face, and there was much rejoicing.

Research Notes
on the Slow, Excruciating,
Bemusing Death of Fun

For the time past of our life may suffice us to have wrought the will of the Gentiles, when we walked in lasciviousness, lusts, excess of wine, revellings, banquetings, and abominable idolatries...

But the end of all things is at hand: be ye therefore sober, and watch unto prayer.

— 1 Peter Chapter 4

"We have to talk," said Yasufumi-sensei, in full-bore more-sad-than-angry mode, "about Clark." He had discreetly summoned four of us to his top-floor office after a general faculty meeting and carefully shut the door.

He elaborated: "A few of our students tell me that they're uncomfortable around him."

He then distributed a two-page handout to the rest of the group, all tenured professors except me.

It was the printout of an email thread, a conversation between Clark, an English teacher on limited contract, and a junior English major who was studying for her credential to teach high school English.

The student had initiated the exchange with a simple class-related question, after which Clark had done his utmost to sustain and deepen it, finally inviting the young lady to go away with him to a three-day academic conference in another city. This exchange had been forwarded to Yasufumi by the student, who was at a loss how to respond to this proposal.

There was more. Of course, there was more—isn't there *always* more with these sorts of things? Another female student had told Yasufumi that Clark's classroom demeanor discomfited her. No details were made available.

"So, what do we do about this?"

"This is very sad news," said the chief of our group.

"Is Clark married?"

"Sad, sad. Just very sad."

I was beginning to think that Clark had strangled the chief's dog.

"Divorced, I think. I know he lives alone."

There ensued much of the sort of argle-bargle that so often ensues when a roomful of heterosexual men wrangle with this sort of issue.

"Someone will have to talk to him."

"I'll do it. I'll talk to him."

Only that last line in this melodrama was mine.

Until this point, I had heard my colleagues' deconstruction of our colleague, Clark, as if it were occurring in a wind tunnel. On this dark December afternoon, the small and stuffy office was made unbearable by the body heat of five full-grown men, all of them beefier than I save Yasufumi, whose Napoleonic stature suited him.

As if the stale air and the topic of conversation weren't discombobulating enough, I was seated next to the extra desk in Yasufumi's office, which, some years earlier, had been *my* office when I was attached to IR: the very same desk atop which I had writhed with the Girlfriend the final time she had bestowed great satisfaction upon me.

No ill consequences, career-wise at least, had befallen me for that long, forbidden relationship; now, the career of a colleague was hitting the rocks and breaking to pieces over matters that, while surely worthy of action, seemed far less egregious than desktop writhing, fraternization-with-NU-chicks-wise.

So then I said: "I've done worse."

—☐—

Ultimately, there was to be no Old White Coot Summit between Clark and me. It was determined that young Yasufumi, not I, would host the uncomfortable sit-down, and that Clark, if contrite, would be allowed to survive the incident.

Normally, I thrill to news of a colleague getting into trouble for overstepping his bounds—who doesn't?—but this... This was nothing so remote from my experience as Russ, the corpulent gaijin nitwit who tried to barter academic credits for oral gratification, or your occasional Japanese lecturer rambling on about naked judges and such. This cut closer to the proverbial bone. Clark's emails read very much like extra-chromosome versions of some of *my* emails.

Why him? Why not me? I threw these questions not at any deity, but rather at the great Hive-Mind of NU women—which, I suppose, is a species of deity after all. In this brave new age of sexual harassment policy, the Hive-Mind seemed to function like The Man Goin' Round Takin' Names in the old Leadbelly tune, randomly bringing the scythe down on some stunned scuzz-ball to my left, then another one to my right, and then hovering away, leaving me unscythed. Given the relative gravity of my sins versus theirs, how could I not feel Survivor's Guilt?

I took the next opportunity to look closely at Clark in search of some insight and regretted doing so immediately, for he was ugly. He was even older than I was, for one thing. By a solid three months. I had taken part in his interview and thus knew his personal data. After he was employed, he was delighted to learn that he and I shared a birth year.

He had piercing, beady, pale blue eyes with enormous bags

under them. For my part, I covered my ageing eyes with cute, round, wire-rimmed glasses, which I took off only in the presence of those I most deeply trusted.* But Clark…those bags… Uncovered, naked to the world… Like a raccoon coming off a meth binge.

Otherwise, he was far fitter than me—spent his weekends on long bike rides through the Kanagawa countryside while I hid behind blackout curtains, moaning and nursing hangovers. His body was Hulk-in-mid-transformation buff. That had to count for something.

So even if I could claim a youthful-appearance advantage over him, it came down to a superior choice of eyewear and a judicious application of Just For Men? Not exactly reassuring.

—▢—

I had a sleepless night on Sunday and went through Monday in a daze. Yasufumi and I had office hour together—or at least we did once he got done with Clark. He wants me to write another damn paper for the journal and says he thinks he could get me appointed as a professor.

I tried to impress on him how easily Friday's discussion on Clark could one day be a discussion about me. I advised him that he might want to distance himself from me for his own sake. He said whatever happened is all in the past and didn't cause any complaints, etc. I said the past has a way of bubbling up…

November 2004

—▢—

* With the Greatest Generation chicks of 2002—Kiko, Nanako, that lot—I used to take off my glasses to punish one of them for errant classroom behavior, peering relentlessly at the miscreant with my vein-striped vampiric orbs until she squealed and begged me to *Cover them up, for God's sake!*

Many years ago, when I suffered delusions of becoming a legitimately published writer, I purchased a registry of American literary agents that listed each agent's preferred genres. A typical entry might read:

Looking for: General fiction, gay/lesbian, historical fiction, horror, romance, women's fiction, biography
Other: No religious works or memoirs, please.

And then there was this odd proviso, which came up not once, but twice:

Other: No accounts of conflicts with faculty colleagues, please.

Who'd have thought that *that* constituted a genre? And yet, there it was. Somewhere, a bookshelf groans under the weight of tomes composed by disgruntled faculty members, as well as those by once-gruntled faculty members who read those accounts, recognized themselves in them, and then felt compelled to fire off their own books in response.

The last thing I wish to do now is contribute to all that. I set out to tell stories about young Japanese women—or, more precisely, about a foreign man's seesaw struggle to cope with his feelings about them—and presumably that is the subject that lured the reader to this work. You are not here to read accounts of lumpy, poorly groomed male academics sitting in small rooms discussing the failings of other lumpy, poorly groomed male academics. In a just world, there is no market for that.

However, it would be the worst sort of elision for me to tell this tale without dragging faculty colleagues into it at some point. It would be like setting a rom-com in the zombie apocalypse without ever showing any zombies.

I'm afraid that my account will be all the more tedious for the fact that I had no "conflicts" per se with Yasufumi, Clark, et al, and yet, through their attitudes and actions and even their kindnesses toward me, my colleagues made sure that I would keenly feel the need to leave NU and never come back.

—◻—

A few years earlier, it had been a rather different story in the old IR department, where some tenured superiors were actively making my life miserable.

Then, one day I was flagged down while riding my bike across campus by a flat-topped youngster who looked like a Japanese exchange student in a 1964 *Archie* comic. He introduced himself in smooth and confident English. He had been wanting to meet me, he said, because he had heard so many students sing my praises, especially regarding my TOEFL classes. And would it be okay if he dropped in the following week to observe part of a day of the intensive course?

I soon learned that Yasufumi had already completed a PhD in English education in Philadelphia, that he spoke flawless, rapid-fire English, and that he bubbled over with ideas for curriculum reform, which he planned to carry out in a new department just then being formed.

After observing my TOEFL class, he suggested that I join him in that department, which would handle English classes for a number of NU departments. When I did not leap at the chance, he dangled the possibility of elective classes that would be open to IR majors, such as the classes through which I would later meet beloved intern Kuni.

"There's a rumor that you're planning to leave Nangaku and go to AU," he observed, with disconcerting accuracy. "Don't you think you'd be happier staying here and working with these students?"

And, well, he had me there.

—◻—

He specialized in qualification courses for the (overwhelmingly female) students who aspired to become K-12 English teachers. He quickly acquired a great deal of influence over this harem, which overlapped to no small extent with my own constituency, the aspiring study-abroaders.

I have elucidated the "one-point-five-year rule" that prevailed in the IR department, under which any lowly English teacher's indiscretion or scandalous act would remain unknown to the out-of-touch power-havers for at least eighteen months—plenty of time to launch a job search. Yasufumi's arrival voided the rule, as demonstrated by the Clark debacle. Henceforth, there would be no grace period between scandal and revelation. Skynet had become self-aware.

"I have, er, done things with NU girls that perhaps go beyond what is acceptable," I said, in a shimmering paroxysm of preemptive euphemism. I wanted him to know this before he went out on a limb to get me into his department.

"I don't know what you're talking about," he said, "but no one has ever complained about you." He knew because he had already checked.

—◻—

During my first year in his department, he seemed to take pleasure in assuring me of my popularity, especially among the female students. "These girls here—they just *love* you!" he would burble, as if this were the most extraordinary thing, like NU girls *en masse* declaring their affection for, say, asbestos.

I smiled and did my aw-shucks thing before realizing that he had subtly set himself up as Supreme Arbiter of Female Student Opinion, and by accepting his praise I had acknowledged him as such. In short, he knew what the Hive-Mind was thinking sooner and better than I ever could. *I've got this whole what-NU-chicks-are-thinking thing covered,* he seemed to be telling me, with a gentle pat. *Don't you trouble your bald old little head over it.*

This, I came to realize at age forty-eight, was what the rest of the world called "office politics." It left an unpleasant, carcinogenic aftertaste, much as asbestos might.

—◻—

Email exchange with the Intern, summer 2005:

Thank you, ohhhhhhh thank you, for pulling me out of the incredibly boring meeting.

Well, "boring" is not really the right word. It was rather heated. When you pulled me out, a fight was about to start between two of my colleagues. When I came back, one of them was dead on the table, and his body had been cut open and his heart was cut out. His enemy had blood all over his face and shirt.

I was glad that I missed watching such a scene.

Anyway, we continued talking about the problem, but we couldn't find a consensus. The dead guy's open eyes were very distracting.

I don't know how long I can continue to teach in Nangaku from now on. As you know, I'm a lover, not a fighter...

After I came home, I ate your cream puff. It tasted full of love, and I forgot the day's terrible events. Thank you.

Me

I haven't known you've had a such rough meeting in Nangaku...
It's so pity thing.
But it's strange because there isn't the department of medical science in

Nangaku...
Why did the professor operate the enemy......?
It's so hot yesterday, so that scenery must had made you cool...

Anyway,I think that professors should be calm in any situation.
I'm a lover, too, so I'm very sad and I'm anxious about you. I earnestly hope that you won't have any such troubles any more.
And of course, also I hope that you continue to teach us in NANGAKU... ;
— ;

Kuni

—◻—

Vernon dropped by my office one day to remind me of a meeting while I was helping an Asada Girl translate her report. Later he said:

"You should be more careful when you're alone with a student in your office."

"What do you mean?"

"You were sitting awfully close to her."

"But...I've known her for years."

In my mind, this excused everything. I did not know what to say in response to the intimation that I had engaged in inappropriate behavior, as there was no precedent.

Oh, being told on this or that occasion "Hey, Muggins, back off!" was old hat, but the telling had always come on the spot from the very girl receiving that behavior. Hearing the same concept channeled through a third party—that did not compute.

A tenure-track professor, Vernon had moved to our new department from the English Department, where he had been a contractee. He was tall and stoop-shouldered, married to a Japanese, and not a Mormon, which was a shame, because he shared with that demographic a knack for awkward attempts at humor. I feel compelled to add that, when not making me feel like an oversexed turd, he was a supportive colleague who later wrote me the most glowing, tear-inducing letter of recommendation I've ever read.

His problem was that he had two daughters who were approaching that terrifying age at which reprehensible men like me would begin judging them at least partly by their appearance. As a result, he had been rendered incapable of sexualizing any NU girl on the rationale that "She, too, is somebody's daughter."

One afternoon, after much cajoling, I was able to wring from him an admission that he at least was aware of the uncommon splendor of our surroundings there at the NU campus, and that he shared my sense of good fortune. But that was as far as he would go down that road.

One had to feel sorry for fathers of daughters, really. How frustrating must it be to come to Nangaku every day and *not* feel free to fantasize? It would be like making serial trips to Lourdes without bathing in its healing waters, or rocketing to the moon and just grabbing some rocks without pausing to take in the splendor of an Earthrise.

The daughterless Yasufumi was much more flexible on such matters. If no one dropped by during our twice-weekly shared office hour, I would expound on which of our students I found most inspiring. He was too dignified, or coy, to go beyond the occasional affirming nod, but always seemed eager to hear my views.

—◻—

I'm not nearly as in danger of falling into sin as I had thought. I think Yuriko just feels sorry for me, regarding me as a lonely middle-aged man, and she is largely correct. Ayana refuses to answer my E-mail, perhaps put off by my offer to massage her injured ankle and then throw in other body parts for no extra charge. It seems my recklessness is exceeded only by my ineptitude. Oh well, at least I've managed to keep my hands off the freshmen for a few weeks.

November 1997

Check out that journal entry plucked almost randomly from the middle of my International Relations years. This is why I trembled before those capricious gods that singled out the likes of Clark while sparing me. This is why, at the height of that discussion over Clark's fate, I had said "I've done worse."

"*What* have you done that's worse?" Vernon had then asked.

"I've, um…taken a lot of girls out to dinner, for one thing."

"Arrrgh…"

"Yes, but nobody has ever complained about you," said Yasufumi—in public, for a change.

And of course, there was that: fifteen years and counting with no complaints apart from those thrown directly in my face in private by gracious, supportive chicks like Kuni and the ex.

But it occurred to me then that lack of complaints doesn't equate with total satisfaction. Sprinkled over those years were vague memories of a girl or two who had been constantly surly toward me for reasons I could not fathom, or a few who had been cordial at first only to cool off as the year wore on. Could my classroom comedic stylings—the long-since discontinued practice of offering birthday kisses and so forth—have caused that? Could some girls have harbored disgruntlement that they kept to themselves, for fear of friction with pro-Muggins classmates?

This was making my head hurt.

—▫—

As previously noted, the group resolved that Yasufumi and not I would talk to Clark. But for the record, here's what I *would* have said to Clark had I drawn the assignment and been able to muster the courage.

Clark… Good God, man. Take a look in the mirror. Can you imagine any twenty-one-year-old wanting a piece of what you see there?

And how dare you be exactly the same age as I am. How dare you, sir! *Do you have any idea what your baggy face does to* my *self-esteem and fantasy life?*

Look, I've been dealing with NU chicks a lot longer than you have. You have to think of them the way you think of blowtorches. With a little experience and proper safety measures, you can have all sort of naughty fun with them. Get drunk and grab them impulsively, and they'll scorch your whole face off. Which, in your case, might be a good start.

And another thing. Whenever we talk about students, you come on all avuncular and say things like, "Oh, yeah, Arisa—she's a good kid" and such. "Kids"—you always use that word.

Now listen: It seems to me that there are exactly two possible mindsets that a male university teacher can possess: The avuncular one where you think of the students as "kids," in which case you block them out of your thoughts forever after—yes, even an electrifying Amazoness like Rina Asai; or the one that regards them as fellow adults, in which case you can go right ahead and imagine showering with them in a business hotel near your academic conference. There is no in-between here, no mixing-and-matching.

But it's not as if you can you make up your mind to be one way or the other. It's no more a choice than gayness versus straightness, or our need to sit down to pee at this age. You know what I mean. We are what we are. No problem so long as you embrace your destiny.

But you! You clearly want to blend kids with shower, and that, sir, is an Abomination in the Eyes of the Lord!

And then I actually imagined myself ending this talk with a stern *Comprende?* until I realized that I was not that big an asshole.

—☐—

But who's to say that I mightn't have evolved into a colleague-scolding, *comprende*-saying, santorum-clogged asshole, given enough time in this environment, given the company I was keeping?

My patron, the boy-king Yasufumi, continued to be a great booster. He compelled me, much against my will, to start writing and publishing papers at the age of forty-eight, the better to sustain my career somewhere else after my NU contract expired. At the same time, he came up with extremely radical plans for curriculum reform that seemed designed to force many part-time English instructors to quit.

His justifications for these schemes gave me chills, like tales of couples who parked in the woods to make out on a moonless night. "If they don't like the new system," he was fond of saying, "they can just walk away."

But he would present these ideas with a squint and a tone so soft and lulling that, had he said, "What we need to do is have every teacher fill his or her butt-crack with peanut brittle just before lessons and then slither across the classroom floor like a landed eel," I would have said, "Oh, yes, let's do that." I came to feel like that Scotsman in Uganda who was befriended by Idi Amin.

—▫—

In summer of the following year—the first year of Kuni's internship—a reporter for the monthly NU propaganda newsletter visited one of my classes for the purpose of cobbling together a fluff piece on NU's mythically popular gaijin English teacher. The reporter later sent an email to thank me for my cooperation and alert me to the possibility of being contacted by the real mass media for follow-up interviews.

In fact, I was already dreading contact from Japanese reporters at that point because my first memoir had been released a few months earlier. I had taken pains to ensure that no PR be done in Japan, but with a title that began *How to Pick Up Japanese Chicks*, well, if I were Fate, I'd swear I was being tempted.

And it would only take one reporter. After that, the pack mentality would set in, and they'd be lined up outside my apartment with the klieg lights, or whatever you call them, and those fuzzy gorilla-dick mikes and everything else. Such were my nightmares in those days, when my subconscious liked to loiter at the intersection of Grandiosity and Paranoia.

—◻—

During my final semester at NU, the provost and vice-provost of that small Midwestern school that Honami had mockingly dubbed "Worthless College" came over to commemorate the fiftieth anniversary of our exchange relationship. As I had become what I believe the French call an *éminence grise* in the realm of NU exchange relationships, I was invited to join the small dinner party in their honor at a ritzy Japanese restaurant near the Tokyo campus.

Whatever wariness I brought to my first-ever close encounter with NU's president, vice-president, and chairman of the board of trustees quickly dissipated when the chairman, a truly greasy eminence from way back, quickly got liquored up, belittled the uncomprehending president in English, cackled at his own mean jokes, then excused himself and fell flat on his face halfway to the restroom. The president, unable to join the English banter, whimpered dejectedly into his beer all night. The VP was actually pretty cool.

It was an instructive evening. For years I had pictured these potentates as shadow-dwelling, black-robed warlocks perched in a gloomy aerie that my imagination appropriated from a particularly over-the-top episode of *Charmed*, observing with displeasure the activities of my peers and me through a crystal ball and debating in ethereal tones and plummy British accents whether or not it was finally time to intervene.

Now, with one foot out the door, I finally saw my masters in all their humanity. Oh, the humanity. The bumbling, liquored-up, neurotic humanity…

The next day, I met the all-female group taking my TOEFL class and gleefully reconstructed the party for them, playing all the roles.

Things that Won't
Happen at RU

Thus Kent, O princes, bids you all adieu;
He'll shape his old course in a country new.

– King Lear

The pictures were from a camera I got for TOEFL Hell. Lots of pictures of
girls I was madly in love with for six days, and now I can't even put names to
their faces. I remember Juri Kato, though. Evidently she was braless, and the
flash allows me to make out the vague outline of her nipples. I have to admit,
this is exciting.

October 2005

After lunch and (often) a nap at my desk, I go off to ... a movie elective,
where I meet even brighter and more eager and more gorgeous people. (Riho
Takeuchi sat in front and treated me to heretofore unimagined acres of
cleavage.) That 90 minutes flies by and then the long, lonely weekend begins.

October 2005

I try to think positive about RU, but Nangaku isn't helping. I always
wake up tired on Friday morning and drag myself off to [NU] English
Communication class, where I'm greeted by bright and eager and (in the
Sociology class, anyway) gorgeous students…. I honestly believe that even at 50

I could manage to have sex with Sae Uchiyama four times in a single night without any chemical aid.

October 2005

—▢—

All the above posts come from the month that I turned fifty years old. This looked to be my final birthday in the nurturing bosom of NU womanhood. In spite of the momentum toward a move to RU, I was applying to other institutions as well, as the following entry makes clear:

Got into the office today around noon because it's pre-application week again for the study-abroad selection. Recent fantasy objects Shion and Riho both dropped by… I had a jolly time trying to get those two to finally settle on a first-choice school. Then I came home and orgasmed ferociously into my sex toy while imagining both of them naked.

Both the "foreplay" in my office and the consummation hours later reinforced the notion of how hard it would be to leave Nangaku, so it is far from today's headline story that TU rejected me. Even Mrs. Muggins said that I would not have been happy with TU girls; that's a great thing for a wife to say.

November 2005

—▢—

TOEFL Hell started yesterday and immediately I felt better. A room full of naked sophomore girls will do that to you. I used to hate everything French including Nangaku French majors, but the Hiroko Ueno-Kimika Sawa tag team has changed all that. They may be the best fantasy tag-team combo since the heyday of Kaori Handa and Michiru Miyata five years ago.

July 2006

Two months later, RU let me know that I had passed my interviews and would be welcome to join them and their dreadful students for a tenure-track position come April. There ensued many sleepless nights.

Nangaku girls have, quite unintentionally, been going out of their way to make me wish that some sort of glitch would arise in the RU application. Classes went well all week. Mitsuki Yamasaki sat in the front row on Monday and shined her headlights at me in a tank-top. The next morning, I indulged myself by naming myself the conversation partner of Saya Wakatsuki, a lush-lipped Soc major designed by God to provoke evil fantasies in middle-aged men. On Tuesday afternoon Runa Amemiya came to my office to be the first of my research volunteers. She performed poorly on the test, but was still wonderfully Runa throughout.

I saw her again in 4ᵗʰ period, and this was where they (Nangaku girls) brought out their big guns. Emino showed up to say that she got the 213 she needs to go to New Zealand, and brought Sawako with her. Their friend Mao (with whom they always engage in faux-lesbian hugging when they get together) announced that she had pulled a 197 out of the blue and was now a UC candidate.

Kuni showed up to get the tape of my conversation with Runa (which she is bound to transcribe for me) and rubbed my head publicly.

Everyone was sharp as tacks in movie class and answered the questions after just one listening.

October 2006

Head-rubbing was, or so I'd like to think, an elder NU woman's way of telling younger NU girls, "This is *my* bald old gaijin. You go find yourselves one of your own. Run along now."

— ¤ —

Ignoring my nightly prayers, the heathen poobahs at RU failed to retract their job offer, but I still had one more cohort of mostly IR-majoring, entirely female study-abroad applicants to abet and to ogle, and I was determined to devote maximum effort to both tasks. The abetting was complicated by major changes in the makeup of the TOEFL test; the ogling was still old-school, though.

What was apt to be my last real Nangaku birthday was a fairly good one—not the greatest by any means, but a good one…Yurika Arai stopped by to give me muffins. I missed Runa, though, who gave me a headband and coffee cup on Tuesday.

October 2006

And Fusami Shinkai, rapidly emerging as the Last Temptation of Josh, got the whole class to sign a big sign-board thing, including a girl that I haven't seen in person since May.

This Fusami started sending me Free Writing some time ago and then segued into chatty Japanese messages, a la You Know Who. [The Girlfriend – Ed] I can't help responding in the same spirit and vaguely flirting—it's what I do. I'm not especially worried about it, though. By the time things might actually heat up, I'll be gone…

October 2006

I felt like shit when class began Saturday, but was buoyed by the turnout… The first ever iBT TOEFL Hell was a horrible bitch to prepare for… but in the end…I survived it, the students seemed to enjoy it, and there was tangible improvement in their scores. On top of that, Sakiko broke out her massive cleavage one last time, even in the middle of December. That was nice of her.

C-chan Nakazato passed the selection to go to Yonsei in Korea and told me on Monday. Later in the week another batch of my darlings will get good news.

December 2006

—◻—

Here end the archives of my encounters with and thoughts about NU girls. My career had another few months to run, but somehow I have managed to lose my entire journal for the year 2007 and thus have no foundation for describing those Final Days. Just as well, I suppose, as I'm guessing those entries were a tad on the maudlin side.

I moved house a week into April, just after RU's 2007 academic year had begun.

In Japan, rentals are unfurnished in the extreme. The curtains, the light fixtures, the air conditioner, even the living room carpet at my apartment in Nangaku Land were all my own and had to be dealt with.

I realized how little renovation I had done in the decade I had lived there. I had not acquired a single new stick of furniture, nor moved any. On some level, I suppose I had thought it sacrilegious to change anything after The Girlfriend walked away back in 2000. Miss Havisham had nothing on me.

I chose to pack the curtains and ask the movers to bring the air conditioner. The carpet? No, it didn't fit the shape of any of my new rooms. I would have to cut it up into small enough pieces to fit into garbage bags and take it out to the curb.

When I started pulling up that carpet, there arose an enormous cloud of dead skin cells, at least some of which had been sloughed off by generations of Nangaku girls dating back to the twentieth century.

Jesus, I said to myself, standing amid the DNA blizzard in the barren apartment, *I have havishammed the shit out of this place.*

Not Quite Friends

No matter how happily a woman may be married, it always pleases her to discover that there is a nice man who wishes that she were not.
—H. L. Mencken

No sooner had I signed in and clipped on my name tag than that old familiar cry of *Muuuggggginnnssss!* rent the air.

It was Midori, entering class of '99. Therefore, I said "Mi-do-ri!" with perhaps more force than those syllables are usually uttered.

"You're here!" she said, upon which note she unceremoniously marched inside my space bubble and stroked my forearm as if to persuade herself of the veracity of her own statement.

"Mi-do-riiiiii…" I bleated. She was tiny and bubbly, and her eye contact had hit my skull like a turkey-baster of cocaine.

"You look just the same!"

"Well, I haven't changed my hairstyle."

"*I* shaved your head once. Remember?"

"Sorry about that."

"What? Why? It was fun!"

—▢—

I have not deigned to introduce the reader to Midori until now. Permit me to rectify the error. She was an IR major whom I befriended through her activities in the very club which had drawn us together again on this very special day.

I remembered her primarily for a rough draft she had asked me to check for an intercollegiate English speech contest, a persuasive address under the title "Let's Use Condoms!" that included some rather graphic details to justify her view.

While return-mailing it, I appended a note praising both her choice of topic and her courage for speaking publicly on the issue. She wrote back to thank me and report that, by the way, she was still a virgin, despite being a junior in college and achingly adorable. I instantly recalled a maritime limerick I had heard somewhere that concluded in the line *Not a bad record for this vicinity.*

My second most vivid Midori-related memory concerned her club's nearly all-female production of *Romeo and Juliet*, highlighted by Mercutio fellating the fiery Tybalt's sword. Midori was not in the cast, but had sat next to me in the NU theater, and had remained admirably restrained at that moment, declining to interrupt the performance to insist that the sword wear a condom.

Now this very same Midori, in a gorgeous blue dress, was stroking my arm and expressing her delight that I should appear at this reunion. This actual physical contact with an actual NU woman for the first time in over five years, however brief, augmented the dizzying sensation of the whole event.

—◻—

In February 2012 the Nangaku English Speaking Association, the club that I had served as advisor throughout my NU career, held a reception at the NU Tokyo Campus to mark their fiftieth anniversary, and someone thought to track me down.

I wavered. Throughout my years of exile, I'd been trying to expunge NU from my mind, for fear that memories of the past would force me to see the present for the desolate Hellscape that it was—not that the present wasn't doing a bang-up job of that on its own. In any event, I had not set foot on NU property for five years and fully intended to extend that record.

But the ESA event would be held on the Tokyo Campus, not the sacred ground of Yokohama, and that made it easier to accept. Tokyo Campus had never seemed to me to be much more than Nangaku's closet, a place in which to cram the offices of the president and the chairman and other such superfluous flotsam.

Once committed to attending the reception, I began prepping with the vigor and rigor I had once brought to my Nangaku classes. I dusted off my student database, an enormous Excel document into which I had input every NU undergraduate I had ever encountered, and did a search for "ESA." Among many other hits, it yielded:

"achingly beautiful ESA heart-throb; was in 'Chicks who Think I'm Groovy' video"
"tiny ESA fairy; h.s. teacher asked her to ride on his back"
"ESA Amazoness; kissed her on b-day"
"ESA baby-doll, shaved head; UC bound"
"ESA; enough energy to heat the whole campus" ($\rightarrow$ Midori)
"short, busty ESA powerhouse"
"slightly bitchy ESA powerhouse"
"tall, confident ESA chick; gave me dead insect"
"ESA; studied abroad. showed lots of cleavage"
"the Hillary of ESA"

The research paid off: when I spied, for example, "big-beaked, pale ESA member" from the entering class of '96, I nailed her name from twenty paces.

— ¤ —

As the next two hours unfolded, other girls did that same space-invading, arm-stroking number on me, including one who doubled as an Asada Girl. I had forgotten how touchy-feely NU girls had tended to be. It had been a while since I had gotten this much physical contact without unfolding my wallet.

There were tales of others who couldn't come to the event because they were off doing business in Singapore or Australia or more obscure foreign ports. One chick was an editor for NHK, the public television of Japan; another translated subtitles for major Hollywood releases.

There were scads of teachers. Someone was getting a master's in English education owing in part to my example. A girl I had helped gain admission to UC Berkeley was unable to attend due to her duties at UN headquarters, for heaven's sake. And so it went, on and on. The maelstrom of attention and news and arm-rubbing fairly made me swoon. Swoon, I say.

— ¤ —

There were current NU undergraduates on hand, too. They lingered discreetly on the fringes of the venue, crow-like in their dark suits. The event culminated with one massive photo op, for which we were herded outdoors into the courtyard under a leaky sky. It was the current students, most of them female, who performed this herding.

I did not exchange words with any of them, these NU women born well into the Clinton Administration, but I certainly checked them out. I was convinced that I could have identified them as NU women even in a neutral venue, like a bullfighting arena or an opium den. They carried that much *je ne sais quoi* in their DNA.

A terrible sadness overcame me when I realized that they would go through all their college years never having been taught by me, adored by me, late-night drunk-texted by me, or otherwise annoyed by me. For my part, I would never walk into a classroom and feel their intelligence radiating at me from every corner, animating me for the ninety-minute adventure in education that lay ahead.

The whole evening reminded me of how rare it had been at NU to walk into a classroom and be able to reasonably suppose myself to be among the top ten brainiest humans present.

These days, in contrast, I get to feel like Stephen Effing Hawking being wheeled into a cageful of hamsters.

—◻—

At my new school, RU, I'm liked but…I'm not *well*-liked. Girls wave to me, smile at me, and, when the moon is in its seventh house and the Santa Ana winds are blowing, one may actually hug me, but nobody tries to pull off my pants around here.

They let me have my very own seminar, though. Most years, though by no means all, I get more applicants than I can take—just like Professor Asada at NU—and must select my students via interviews, and in this matter the old lion's experience has informed me. When any female applicant interviews to join the seminar, I insist that a current female member sit in and then let her rule my judgment.

Not that there is all that much temptation, mind you. I recall times during my NU career when I would absently scan the campus and wonder, "Say, whatever happened to ugly Japanese girls? Did God just stop making them?" Suffice it to say that the move to RU tied up this loose end for me quite neatly.

One occasionally runs across an RU girl who is as sharp as the average NU chick, and another who is as pretty as the average NU chick, and still another who is as affectionate as the average NU chick, but one never quite gets the beauty, brains, and benevolence bundled onto a single device. RU girls are like methadone, fraught with just enough of the active ingredients I crave to hold off withdrawal and death without providing any high or sense of danger. I suppose this bland sensation is akin to what most chaps my age get from seeing their grandchildren.

It's quite all right so long as I succeed in banishing the past from my mind and avoid making comparisons unprofitable to RU girls, but then…Facebook. Facebook and its goddamned relentless encouragement to "Find Friends" and "Add" them.

249

—☐—

The morning after the ESA reunion, I received a friend request from Midori. My Facebook presence is not my real name, nor even "Josh Muggins," but an even faker fake name. *Never underestimate the sleuthing skills of the NU girl,* I thought, before realizing that I had probably drunkenly told Midori my Facebook identity. In any event, the friend request set me off.

—☐—

It set me off, and not for the first time.

Lord knows I have tried not to trawl for Nangaku chicks online, not so much because the practice goes by unflattering names like "cyberstalking" but because it has tended to leave me drained and depressed—the whole business of comparing the present and past again, don't you see.

But at 1 a.m. on a Sunday morning, what else do you have to do but type in so-and-so's name, but that doesn't work because it's a common name—there's a million of those—so you try her friend instead, and that works, and you see what she's up to and then you check out *her* friends, and oh, there's the other one, and then you go to *her* friends and *her friend's* friends and so on and so forth down the Facebook rabbit-hole.

And you're thinking, *Wow, looks like everybody's having a swell time without me,* and then you remember that the whole point of Facebook is to let everybody *seem* to be having a swell time no matter how crappy their lives may be—that if Kurt Cobain were alive today, he'd be cheerfully showing you the lovely paella he had for lunch and you would say, "Gosh, I sure envy Kurt's swell life."

Of course, there are some who actually employ the privacy options. "Do you know Ruriko?" I am asked. It is a good question, as more than two decades have passed since she yawned erotically on my debut album and I publicly outed her as a serial eyebrow plucker. "To find out what she shares with friends, send her a friend request!"

—¤—

That "Add Friend" button, it just hovers there before your eyes—oh how it hovers!—begging you to just slide that mouse pointer over there—how little effort it would take!—and make a click that would set in motion an irreversible chain of events. It is the most despicable invention of my adult lifetime. With a few keystrokes and clicks, one can now do what once required a fat checkbook and Philip Marlowe: track down old acquaintances whether they want to be tracked down or not.

Yes, oh yes, I would like to add-friend you, and after that, I would like to add-so-much-more you. And where would that lead? And what good could that possibly do you? Or me, for that matter? No, if I yearn to feel close to those girls again or wallow in memories, better to channel that energy into something less intrusive to them, more cathartic for me. Like this book.

But on a certain type of winter night, with the wind howling and Christmas looming and my iTunes holiday playlist surging into the headset and no nearby family to call my own…

—¤—

…Well, well, well, there's Michiru Miyata, in her late 20s now, throwing her hair back, with some white Mediterranean villas facing the ocean in the background, *pa-rum-pa-pum-pum*…

There's Mirai in full riding regalia, smilingly leading a gigantic steed toward an afternoon of hedge-leaping, *pa-rum-pa-pum-pum*. You'd think she'd have married Prince Harry over there in England or something by now. Maybe she did; I don't pretend to keep up on that crap.

There's an International Relations girl named Sena, not previously mentioned in this report—there were just so many, don't you see, so very very many—standing proudly at the back of some neat but overcrowded classroom, beaming, with dozens of African schoolboys staring toward the camera, some apprehensive, some smirking impishly: *What child is this, who, laid to rest...*

Here's another chick standing proudly in front of a group of Indian girls around age nine gathered in front of their school, the students showing off their multicolored native garb, Terumi never more alive than in this moment as one of the girls extends a bony arm to squeeze her shoulder: *Whom angels greet with anthems sweet...*

Kiko, who cleaned my fridge and mixed me lethal cocktails that glorious long-ago afternoon, perhaps went into hostessing, a profession with an expiration date roughly equivalent to that of Pringles chips. I had hoped for something better for her, but she seems happy enough in her Facebook photos, most of which depict her using her earnings on various jaunts to tropical climes with like-minded and like-bodied female friends. *I'll be home for Christmas, you can plan on me...*

Yes, this is the Land of Facebook, so smiling faces would seem to mean little. But I click through these photos on a drunken winter night wanting, so very much wanting to believe, and thus *do* believe in their contentment.*

Here's Rikako, Kiko's Greatest Generation classmate whom I once asked about the relevance of a man's size, on a trip with coworkers to Bali. These photos are dated February 2011, just a month before the great earthquake/tsunami/radiation trifecta that irrevocably altered all our lives, and I can't discern what happened to her after

---

* And so long as they keep presenting themselves in the fizzy, upbeat world that is Facebook, I figure they're doing okay. It's when they stop posting there and descend into the bleak netherworld of Twitter, from whose bourn no traveler returns, that I will fear for them.

that. But back in the blissful ignorance that was February 2011, she is dancing, drinking, smooching, and just having the time of her life, *make the yuletide gay…*

Joyful all ye nations rise! kicks in and tickles my medulla just as I'm zooming in on a picture of Nao Oizumi at some species of festival in some unspecified foreign land, decked out in a motley toga and crown of flowers like Aphrodite or some goddam thing, her huge grapefruit-accommodating mouth wide open in an unguarded moment of pure joy, a moment made possible entirely by *ME!* By *ME,* I keep telling myself! *I* made this magnificent photo possible. *I* made this magnificent young woman. But of course, I did not. My meager contribution would count itself lucky to scrounge a Best Supporting Actor nom from the Academy of Nao Oizumi Arts and Sciences…

In some Facebook profile photos, I find former lust-objects posed with bald, flailing, unpredictable, boob-obsessed creatures of their own making, which, I suppose, explains why they have no further use of me. Ryoko, Kiko's one-time sidekick, is among these. Shojo M claims to have a baby without ever having been married, but there is no photographic evidence, so she's either lying or she has one of those *Eraserhead* babies…

Beyond that tidbit, I'm not revealing anyone's present-day status. Quoting their decades-old emails without permission is one thing, but even I have to draw a line somewhere.

—□—

Teaching English in a Japanese university is, to appropriate one American philosopher's assessment of cocaine, a hell of a drug.

Teaching English at that very special juncture of time and place that was turn-of-the-millennium Nangaku was that and so much more. It was to dwell within a constant tension between lusting and loving, between the will to educate and the need to ejaculate. It was the thrill of creating and sustaining a wonderful, improbable *we* with a type of human with whom—superficially at least—one had

253

nothing whatsoever in common; and then starting all over from zero in the springtime.

Regardless of all that has happened since, I still don't regret leaving when I did. I was fifty-one years old, for heaven's sake, and the Greatest Generation—the lot who had descended on my apartment for marathon parties at which we shared customized cocktails and antidepressants—had graduated the previous spring. True, I would be leaving Kuni unattended and unemployed for the final year of her student life, but she would muddle through with her multitude of friends and her UC boys.

Leaving when I did meant that no Nangaku girl would ever see me doddering and dotty or hauled up on charges, and that, for my part, I would never see any of them falling in love with one of my successors, some young crocodile-wrestling Aussie buck with hair and charisma and all that crap; or, rolling their eyes over being stuck in "the old guy's class."

I wonder what memories of me live on in the minds of Nangaku chicks. Given how confused I was, and still am, about the nature of my affection for them, I cannot imagine how discombobulating the experience must have been for the recipients of that affection. Beyond being simply a collection of old stories I wanted to tell before shuffling away, this book is, I suppose, a stab at figuring that out. But given that there were a couple thousand of them, each with her own way of processing creepy-white-guy stimuli, that now seems a fool's errand.

To be sure, there is a large buffet of shared experiences—some lovely, some not so much—for them and me to select from; but the memories I choose to scoop onto my plate are about as close to perfect as our local gods—notorious haters of perfection in mortal art—will permit.

WELL, THEN...

Reader—and at this point, the singular form isn't really a rhetorical device, as I suspect you're the only one left—much has changed in the eleven years since my first memoir on the subject of my interactions with the young women of Japan went to press back in 2004. You don't hear nearly so much from Saddam Hussein or Ashlee Simpson these days, for one thing, and how about that Bill Cosby, eh? Raise your hand if you saw *that* coming back in pre-Katrina times. But all that is neither here nor there.

Of greater interest to me—being, as I am, a writer or something—are the changes that have been wrought upon the English language. Perhaps terms such as "Asian fetish" and "white male privilege" had already been coined back in the early Aughts, but holed up in my lead-lined lair over here in Yokohama I managed to remain blissfully ignorant of them.

"Asian fetish," I gather, refers to the sexual preference of some Caucasoid or Negroid males for females either raised in East Asian countries or of said ancestry. To this the aging expat nods and says, "Ah, yes, and when I was a wee lad Stevie Wonder was wont to sing of Jungle Fever. Some people just have a natural urge to mate with a particular other race. And more power to 'em, right? Maters gonna mate, as the young folks say!" But a Google search reveals that in most instances *Asian fetish* is used *pejoratively*, to suggest something shallow or incomplete about the afflicted party. What's up with that?

"White male privilege" is a concept more easily grasped—something that, indeed, I can almost imagine myself sinking my teeth into in some parallel universe where I had chosen to live out my days amongst the Whites. But I did not so choose, and I do wish that some kind soul would point out to my faculty colleagues that Muggins-sensei is a certified White Male™ and thus entitled to privileges. Just, you know, for those two or three times a year when I have something to say at a meeting.

And then we have "trigger warnings" and "microaggressions" and *Jumping Jehoshaphat*, Reader, what has the world come to? We creatures of 2004 could not foresee Twitter, let alone these Twitter Mobs they have nowadays, hungrily lurching hither and yon toward the sound of any perceived offense, no matter how inadvertent or trivial.

You may well wonder why, in such a climate, an elderly white male writer would choose to write and publish a memoir of his interactions throughout middle age with young Japanese females, replete with explicit descriptions of the workings of his warped hetero mind, when simply stating the book's concept that way might get him into all sorts of trouble.

And Reader, the answer to that question is: I don't quite recall. I started on this project about four years ago and now I'm turning sixty, for heaven's sake. Retirement from both my day job and from writing is imminent. It's a minor miracle when I can find where I left my hearing aids, never mind dredging up ancient book-concept motivations.

But maybe, just maybe it had something to do with old writers liking new challenges. Some may aim to compose a whole novel without using a particular vowel, for example. Perhaps I'm exploring whether or not a topic that is inherently viewed as creepy by a significant chunk of the Anglophone world can somehow be rendered not merely non-creepy, but uplifting and entertaining.

Look, you can't write a book like this—or any kind of book, I suppose—from a defensive mindset and then expect it to be any good (he said, somewhat defensively). So I can't honestly say that I went out of my way to avoid any content that might cause offense. But I *can* honestly say that not a single phrase was included herein for the purpose of poking a stick at any particular group.*

My hope is simply that the reader will see life in Japan or the Western expat experience from a novel perspective through this book and have some fun along the way. At the very least, there must be some anthropological value in watching a clueless twentieth-century Caucasaurus stagger blindly through an alien culture in an alien century. Right?

---

* Well, okay: that swipe I took at the Kevin Costner demographic was entirely deliberate. (For the record, I like Kevin.)

Acknowledgments

All wording in the boxed snippets concerning the Clinton-Lewinsky affair is my own and the factoids contained therein, including excerpts from testimony, are a matter of public record available online and in many publications. That said, it would be disingenuous and an extreme breach of etiquette on my part to fail to acknowledge with gratitude the concise timeline compiled by *Time* magazine reporters for their September 21, 1998 edition and another timeline, the authorship of which I could not determine, which I accessed at the following address associated with City University of New York: http://academic.brooklyn.cuny.edu/history/johnson/clintontimeline. htm.

As always, Gary Pettis provided invaluable encouragement and advice. Bo Mak did the wonderful cover art. Most of my colleagues at "R. University" have accepted me for the person that I am and have not so overburdened me that I could not find time to write this book. All of the above have my gratitude.

Above all, Mrs. Muggins continues to grant me the freedom to live my own life while I give her the same. If there's a greater expression of love than that, I don't know what it is.

Confessions

The anecdotes concerning the Christmas Eve makeup class and the reunion where I ran into Midori were previously published on joshmuggins.com.

When the cashier at my local supermarket offers me free disposable chopsticks, I sometimes accept them even though I'll be eating at home where I could easily use my regular chopsticks.

Chicklist

In lieu of a bona fide Index, please refer to this table to sort out the women referred to in this opus. Alphabetical order of given name. Major characters in boldface.

Ai Enoki	Greatest Generation, #9 on the List	24, 27
Aika Matsuo	Greatest Generation	8
Airi Onda	Madoka classmate	144
Aki Mino	Lap-sitter, failed head-shaver	74, 163-64
Akiko	Possessor of exciting padded body	71
Akimi Torii	Muggins impersonator	111
Anna	Swooning participant in cheesy video	167
Arisa	Intern acquaintance	217
Asako Kubo	Head-shaver	166
Asami Ohashi	Cool beauty who overcame death of parents	137
Asuka Yamamoto	*Ur*-head-shaver	162
Ayako	Greatest Generation food spitter-outer	29, 41
Ayana	Acerbic friend of Naomi Murata; featured in other memoir	83, 87, 233
Azusa Hoshino	Duet recording participant	102-03
C-chan Nakazato	Study-abroad applicant	242
Chiaki Kamei	Object of shirtless handjob fantasy	181
Chieko	Horrible baker	66-67
Chika	**Christmas pageant tyrant**	**149-53**
Chinatsu	Cheesy video participant	167

Ikumi Suematsu	Backing vocalist	168
Izumi Hatayama	Dead boyfriend haver	10, 145
Junko	Giver of ominous-sounding praise	124-25
Juri Kato	Possibly braless study-abroad candidate	177, 181, 239
Kaho Takino	Affectionate English Speaking Association president	77
Kaori Handa	Fantasy object	240
Kayo Mitani	Greatest Generation, seeker of kissing advice	24, 39, 41
Kazane Orimo	Study-abroad candidate; fantasy object	221
Kazue Inoue	Yuriko sidekick and music critic	96
Kazumi Ando	Greatest Generation, Muggins fart inducer	8, 24, 27
Kazuyo Mashiko	Sphinx-like drinking buddy	119, 122-24
Kiko Kogawa	**Greatest Generation; possessor of cleavage worthy of academic study; puller-offer of Muggins' pants; #1 on List, later demoted**	**4-6, 8, 23-24, 41, 145, 252-53**
Kimi	Friend of Toko; erotic yawner; sender of chocolates	50-51, 53-58, 61, 68
Kimika Sawa	Fantasy tag-team partner of Hiroko Ueno	240
Kondo-san	Petite nemesis of Toko	55-56
Kotoko Inaba	**Long-time erotic email correspondent**	**11-19, 181-82, 197**
Kuni Bando	**Last Intern; stalker of UC boys; light of Muggins' pathetic life in twilight years**	**185-222, 229, 231-32, 234, 235, 241, 254**

Madoka Wada	"Shojo M"; serial grabber of Muggins' buttocks and classmate's bosoms	126-46, 149, 253
Mai Onuma	Great Woman of Nangaku; Sexual Harassment Questionnaire consultant	84-85, 104, 106-10
Maki Migita	Author of moving Christmas essay; Asada Girl	142-43, 159-60
Mamiko	Greatest Generation; #5 on List	26, 41
Mana Katsuki	Great Woman of Nangaku	89
Manami Yagi	**Muggins-hating law major**	**174-77**
Manatsu Mori	Fantasy object; study-abroad candidate, frenemy of Last Intern Kuni	197, 200, 204-06, 210, 212, 215-16, 218-22
Mao	Study-abroad candidate, faux lesbian	241
Masami	Live concert impresario and backing vocalist	154-55
Mayumi Nishida	Fantasy object	91
Michiko Sunagawa	aka "The Girlfriend," "the ex" (featured in other memoir)	34, 102, 111-13, 118, 136, 225, 234, 242-43
Michiru Miyata	Fantasy object and Facebook user	240, 251
Midori	English Speaking Association speech-writer and condom expert	245-47, 250
Mieko Iwasawa	Album co-producer and backing vocalist	100-03, 111, 113
Mihoko Kano	Star of cheesy video project; fantasy object	77, 167
Mika	Greatest Generation, helper of immigrants	23
Mio Horii	*Ur*-head-shaver	162
Mirai	Study-abroad candidate and fantasy object; later, equestrian	197, 213-15, 217, 220-21, 251

Rina Asai	Study-abroad candidate and fantasy dream team partner of Ena Yuge	180-84, 234
Risa Yamanaka	Birthday kiss recipient	90
Runa Amemiya	Study-abroad candidate; research subject; Muggins head-rubber	217, 241-42
Ruriko	**Erotic yawner; eyebrow plucker; *Ur*-Asada Girl; fantasy object**	**50-51, 53-54, 61-65, 68, 71, 155-59, 250-51**
Ryoko	PR maven for Kiko Kogawa's cleavage; proud Facebook mom	24, 253
Sachiyo	Token ugly girl in Toko orbit; Designated Eater of awful festival food	54-58, 63, 66
Sae Uchiyama	Study-abroad candidate and fantasy object	240
Sakiko	Study-abroad candidate and fantasy object	242
Sanae Kayama	Accidental Muggins cock-toucher	115
Saori Fukushi	Cooker of Italian dinner	112
Satchan Fukazawa	Mac user	77
Satsuki Mori	**Beloved album co-producer and backing vocalist; harsh critic of teacher-student affairs**	**88, 100-03, 111, 113-14**
Sawako	Study-abroad hopeful, faux lesbian	241
Sawayaka (Sayaka) Akiba	Backing vocalist and braces-wearing forbidden fruit	54, 56-58, 61, 63-64
Saya Wakatsuki	Charming Sociology major	241
Sayuri	Chestily memorable classmate of Toko	53

Yayoi Shimamura	Greatest Generation; #2 on List, later #1; late-night phone companion; near-miss affair partner	9, 23, 30-41
Yu	Greatest Generation; #3 on List	24
Yui	Studious faux friend of Madoka Wada	130, 132, 134
Yuika Sekine	Sexually mature freshman	99
Yuka Oh	Study-abroad candidate and fantasy object	179
Yuki Sawada	Chronic cleavage displayer	77
Yukiko Takahashi	Example of "ripe" girl	77
Yukino Tsuino	Incompetent arm wrestler	111
Yumiko	Head-shaver and Tom Cruise fan	74-75
Yuri	Head-shaver	163
Yurika Arai	Birthday muffin-giver	242
Yuriko	Album co-producer and duet partner; Muggins nonsexual harassment victim	77, 87, 90, 96, 109-10, 233

And here are the young gentlemen.

Akio Iida	Seeker of girl-getting advice; accursed deflowerer of Madoka Wada	120-22, 144-45
Atsushi Ito	Study-abroad candidate	181
Daimu	Asexual head shaver	164
Dan	Astute Westernized commentator on Japanese culture	105-06
Goro Watanabe	Preposterous, unfocused follower of Madoka Wada; garlic aficionado; kisser of Muggins	133-35, 138, 139-41, 143-44, 146

Sho Saito	Victim of *quid pro quo* sexual harassment for grade	144
Takafumi Rokuhara	Simulated anal intercourse partner	123
Takuro Fujita	Random guy in class	102
Toru	Greatest Generation; hugely appetited and sometimes pantsless	27, 39
Toshio	Party organizer and potential cellmate	174
Tsuneo Moriyama	Greatest Generation; Yayoi associate	9
Yasushi Senda	Volleyball team organizer and violator of Muggins' mouth	21
Yu-chan Funada	Birthday kisser	89
Yudai	Vulcan-like pal of Last Intern Kuni	196-97, 199-202, 204, 210-215, 217-19
Yuichiro Sakamoto	Towering, filter-less would-be gigolo	178-79
Yuta Ichihara	Violent party attendee	91

Last and least, the colleagues.

Asada	Collector of hot International Relations seminar students	68, 96, 155-60, 232, 247, 249
Clark	Author of disturbing emails to female student	224-228, 230, 233-34
Furman	Dwarfish and stealthy IR supervisor	88
Hogan	IR colleague, fellow Christmas pageant victim	149-53
Russ Fullington	Fatted sacrifice to sexual harassment policy	104, 226

Teddy	Oversexed cautionary tale from Muggins' university days	46
Todd Plotz	Maoist radical much despised by Kuni's cohort	38, 41, 201-02, 204
Vernon	Daughter-having guardian of NU females' virtue	232-34
Yasufumi	Power-mad Muggins patron	177, 224-30, 233-35

www.ingramcontent.com/pod-product-compliance
Lightning Source LLC
Chambersburg PA
CBHW030107070426
42448CB00036B/313